AF265386

NOTES

NOTES

Why? Because we give a "f" ---->

When we say we give a "f" we really mean it. We give a whole lot of "f"s. Which is fun in the wake of the success of the book ***The Subtle Art of Not Giving a F*ck.*** Which, one powerful message from the book was to pick the things that you really do give a "f" about and let go of allllllll the rest. We each get to choose our challenges. So, here's what we give a "f" about when it comes to **"f"ashion** and yes, we are up for the **challenges** that come along with exposing the truth.

FABRIC FIRST

FARM TO FIBER

FOOD TO FIBER

FIELD TO FABRIC

BTL'S FAB 5 FABRICS

FARM TO FASHION

FABRIC FACTORIES

F'ED UP FASHION 5

FUR FREE

FASHION FINDS

FASHION FORWARD

FASHION FIELD TRIPS

UN"F"ING UP FASHION

AND A"FF"ORDABLE FASHION

The #1 thing people are looking for in the clothes that they purchase in general is affordability – sustainable or not.

A"ff"ordable has two "f"s in it so it counts double. ;)

HOW TO SHOP FOR SHI(*F*)T

The shopping guide of healthier fashion for any budget!

TARYN HIPWELL

KAREN HOUSEL & NICHOLAS BROWN

Beyond the Label is a project of Creative Visions, a non-profit exempt from federal income tax under Section 501(c)3 of the Internal Revenue Code. All contributions are tax-deductible to the extent permitted by law.

Written by: Taryn Hipwell

Co-produced by: Karen Housel, Nicholas J. Brown

Edited by: Caroline Pham, Veronica Ko

Copyright Edited by: Sally Glass

Cover Artists: Sinjun, Allison Sherman

Book Layout & Graphics by: Allison Sherman

Graphics by: Maggie Pa

Photos by: Janell Hipwell Photography, Michael Hansel, Kritina Sado, and photo contributions made by Style Profile experts, SUSI, and Groceries Apparel

Student contributions: Colorado State University student, Kristin Breakell for T-shirt Poster-Graphics

ISBN: 978-0-692-96870-3

CHAPTERS

BREAK THE CYCLE.
CLOSE THE LOOP.

INTRODUCTION

Fashion is one of the most toxic industries in the world, though its ranking is highly debated amongst other top polluting culprits – agriculture, oil and gas, electricity and heat, transportation, and livestock industries. This list may vary depending on the expert you ask, although fashion is widely believed to hover around the second-place spot. *It's not exactly the type of thing you want to be known for.* What sucks even more is that the fashion industry contributes to all the other mentioned offenders!

Today, many people are familiar with the concept of "farm-to-table," a movement that offers hungry shoppers a window into where their food comes from and how it's produced. Initially the concept was that food was grown, picked, prepared, set on the table, and then the consumer would eat a meal with the farmer – truly clean eating! With that in mind, we'd like to introduce you to "farm-to-fashion" – a healthy fashion movement for shoppers to better understand not only what their clothes are made of, but where and how the materials are grown and processed. Meeting the designers, seamstresses, and farmers behind our clothing gives us the opportunity to learn how natural fiber is made into fabric, and innovative fabric technologies from textile experts. This enables us to make better decisions about your clothing consumption. Connecting with fashion makers shifts our relationship with clothing.

The fashion industry may have an appetite for destruction, but that doesn't mean we have to contribute to it. One clear difference between the food and fashion industries is that food biodegrades, but most fashion does not. Let's start a clean fashion movement together.

*"The fashion and food industries are connected. All industries that grow plants should stop f'n up soil and water systems, and avoid using toxic pesticides. Picking clothing is just like picking fruit. There is a huge difference between **clean organic methods** and **toxic chemical farming** methods, which **affects millions** of people along the supply chain, including you, "the shopper." Choosing what you wear should be as easy as **checking a nutrition label** and **trusting notable certifications**, just like food."*

— Ron Finley, the "Gangsta Gardener," former fashion designer, TED speaker, and founder of The Ron Finley Project

WHY IS FASHION TOXIC AND UNSUSTAINABLE?

Water use? Chemicals? Textile waste? How does it affect the people that make your clothes? And how does it personally affect you, the shopper?

Here are a few initial references to let us know that an honest, solution-based shopping guide is needed.

——— WHAT'S IN THE NEWS? ———

"Are There Toxic Chemicals in Your Yoga Pants? "
— TheTruthAboutCancer.com

"How Environmental Toxins Harm Women's Reproductive Health"
— LiveScience.com

"American Airlines attendants say new uniforms make them sick, demand 'full recall'"
— USAToday.com

"Ommm -- Your Yoga Pants Are Polluting The Oceans -- Ommm"
— Huff Post

"80,000 chemicals in commerce are free to be used without regulation."
— Unacceptable Levels (film)

PREFACE

Beyond the Label (BtL), founded by Taryn Hipwell, started as a partnership with TEDxLA to educate Angelenos about the true health, social, and environmental costs of their fashion purchases. BtL is now a charitable organization that encourages shoppers to consider, **"What's in my tee?"** to think about what a T-shirt is made of, how it affects you, the workers, and the world we live in.

#MakeShiftHappen

The How to Shop for Shi(f)t guidebook's purpose:

- ○ Introduce better shopping habits, helpful resources, and an understanding of what clothes are made of

- ○ Enable shoppers to ask important questions like: How do my clothes affect the health of my family and myself, the people who make my clothes, and the world that we live in?

- ○ Provide an introduction to fashion-related pollution problems by spotlighting chemicals used and waste created in the making of a garment

- ○ Teach shoppers what to look for, where to find it, and how to use their newfound knowledge to influence the fashion industry

- ○ Offer tools and terms for shoppers to share the exciting things they've learned

- ○ Empower shoppers to #MakeShiftHappen

"Your **clothing should reflect your values** *as well as your aesthetic, and there are so many ways to find great* **sustainable brands** *that align with those values, from websites to e-zines and newsletters to social media feeds and apps – all within your budget."*

– Sass Brown, founding dean of the Dubai Institute of Design and Innovation.

Beyond the Label holds events at a variety of prestigious festivals, universities, and conferences, where attendees who are newly educated about the dark side of the fashion industry constantly ask our team: **"What should I look for?"** and **"Where can I find it?"**

Through years of experience and research, we've realized that there are a wide range of shopping habits and self-expressive senses of personal style. In this guidebook, we tap the deep well of knowledge from leading global fashion experts, and present inspirational style profiles from an incredible group of ethical, sustainable, vegan, "recycle-a-holic," and minimalist shoppers. Hopefully, they will help illustrate positive practices you can embrace to influence the world through what you choose to buy and wear.

In a later chapter, to answer Beyond the Label's core question of **"What's in my tee?"**, we'll dive into the details of 10 carefully selected T-shirts. We'll take a look at the types of fibers used, and where they were made – all to better educate you about transparency, supply chains, healthy or "clean" fashion, and the purpose of each material. Ultimately, our goal is to give you, as a shopper, a more informed explanation of exactly what you're paying for when you shop.

BTL'S MEASURES OF RECOGNITION

Yay! If you see a "Yay!" written in small, bold writing within the guidebook, this is our way of giving special recognition to brands, organizations, and people that are up to something awesome!

Example: Yay! The "O" in Beyond the Label has an opening. This signifies: "Break the Cycle" and "Close the Loop." Traditional fashion is a broken linear cycle where clothing is made with the intention of being thrown away. Innovative fashion that is made with a circular reuse and recycle system in mind diverts and reduces chemicals from soil and water systems and waste from landfills.

Fashion Pollution

Chemicals
o Dyes
o Fibers
o Bleach, Detergents, Pesticides...

Waste
o Biodegradable waste
o Non-biodegradable virgin waste
o Non-biodegradable recyclable waste

Fashion Solutions

Innovative Textiles
o Reduce water usage & pollution
o Reduce waste
o Reduce cancer

Buying Resale
o Reduces chemical usage
o Reduces waste
o Diverts clothing from landfills

CHAPTER 1:

Why We Give a "F"

Personal Statements from the ***Beyond the Label Team***

RECAP OF WHY WE GIVE A "F":
A"ff"ordable Fashion - the #1 aspect shoppers seek
Fashion Forward - style, brands, and self expression
Fashion Finds - secondhand clothing and the reduction of textile waste
Fur Free - vegan textiles and toxic chemicals in fabric
Fair Trade/Fair Labor/Fair Wages - safe, healthy, and fairly paid environment

FABRIC FIRST

We'd love shoppers to think: "What's in my tee?"

Fab 5 Fabrics - fabulous fabric options to look for
F'ed up Fashion 5 - chemicals in fabrics to avoid
Farm to Fiber - natural, organic, and biodegradable fibers
Food to Fiber - reducing landfill waste by converting food to fiber
Fascinating Fabric Factories - the fabric life cycle and circular economy begins here
Farm to Fashion - meet the makers and learn about the processes
Un-F the Fashion Industry - you have the power!

Beyond the Label will address the concept of

"WHAT'S IN MY TEE?"

**several times throughout the book.
Here's why:**

Yes, this means the pores on your butt do, in a way, eat your underwear. Freaky, right!?

In the *How to Shop for Shi(f)t* guidebook, we'll differentiate between "body-edible" fibers and "mouth-edible" fibers. For now, consider that the biggest difference between "you are what you eat" and "you are what you wear" is that you don't see people eating plastic.

Do you know how to read the care label in your T-shirt?

MACHINE WASH NORMAL
TUMBLE DRY LOW
NON-TOXIC DETERGENT
REMOVE PROMPTLY
NO BLEACH

MADE WITH LOVE IN
LOS ANGELES

NUTRITION FACTS

Serving Size
Serving per Container

Amount per Serving	
Calories	Calories from Fat
	% Daily Value*
Total Fat	
Saturated Fat	
Cholesterol	
Sodium	
Total Carbohydrate	
Dietary Fiber	
Sugar	
Protein	
Vitamin A	Vitamin C
Calcium	Iron

A care label is a guide to your clothing, just like a nutrition label is for food. Fabric content, country and city of origin, and special care instructions just aren't enough. Different people value different things when it comes to what they put in their mouths — such as calories, fat, and vitamins. What would the world be like if everyone knew how to assess their tee based on a care label the same way they can assess a bottled tea based on a nutrition label?

(Example: Not all ingredients are created for your health and wellness. Did you know that corn syrup is added to almost everything to trick your brain into thinking you're hungry?)

What to remember when seeking out a healthy T-shirt (or almost anything else you wear):

- Fibers that make up the fabric of your garment are ***ingredients.***
- Chemicals added to alter the state of fabric are ***additives.***
- Clothing items styled to create healthy, sustainable looks based on personal taste create the ***recipe.***

Fashion didn't always contribute negatively to human and environmental health. There was a time when humans made their own clothes from natural fibers and their own dinners from natural foods. Granted, our early ancestors didn't have much of a choice — but now we do. Consider that some CEOs of giant companies intentionally make products that undisputedly contribute to and cause health issues, which in turn contributes to an ever-churning healthcare machine. Whether toxins are added intentionally to harm your health or not, brands that use toxic chemicals do not have your best interest at heart. Similarly, the end goal for many fashion brands is not great quality, but rather profit, which they accomplish by cranking shit out (and by "shit", I mean shitty, toxic, intentionally disposable clothes).

How to Shop for Shi(f)t was created help shoppers shop for self-express-worthy affordable clothes with intention and learn to invest in healthier pieces, while being mindful of fast fashion budgets. The more shoppers learn about new, cleaner technologies in fashion, the more it becomes common knowledge, and the bigger the fire grows under brands' butts to improve. When shoppers demand and articulate exactly what they are willing to spend money on, brands make changes to make money. Many fashion companies won't be happy about the truth bombs being dropped in this book, but *How to Shop for Shi(f)t* will ask all brands of all sizes: "Will you choose to make significant shifts to create healthier products or not?"

BE DISRUPTIVE. QUESTION THE NORM.
WE HAVE THE POWER!

CALLS TO ACTION

SMELL AND ITCH
INFORM US of items that smelled toxic or you had a reaction to, so that we can research and share what the issue may be. Go to LABeyondtheLabel.com.
#SMELLANDITCH

WEAR AND TEAR
CALL OUT shitty items you wore less than 10 times before you had to toss them.
#WEARANDTEAR

LOVE AND LAST
POST pictures of pieces that have lasted past 30 wears that you love.
#LOVEANDLAST

MAKE IT LAST
POST pics of pieces that you have DIY-ed.
#MAKEITLAST

#MAKESHIFTHAPPEN

Letter from Taryn Hipwell
Founder of Beyond the Label

- **Do I think "fast fashion" (disposable, unethically-made, cheap clothes) is going to go away?** Not anytime soon.

- **Do I think fast fashion brands can suck less?** Yep.

- **Am I still going to acknowledge that some fast fashion brands are making an effort to include more sustainable fabrics and reduce toxic chemicals?** Yep.

- **Why do I care about this?** I think it should be a human right to not be exposed to toxic chemicals (pesticides, bleach, detergents, mordants, dyes, formaldehyde, arsenic, etc.) used in the making of conventional cotton, polyester and other conventional natural and synthetic fabrics. I think neighboring communities shouldn't have to drink or bathe in toxic water due to unregulated chemical dumping and pesticide runoff in their water supply. Yes, this is some heavy shit, but I believe you can handle the truth. *How to Shop for Shi(f)t* will introduce you to some of the most innovative new fabric technologies, life hacks, and cool shifts in fashion so you can join in on the movement.

Change does not happen overnight. Eating, building buildings, and even car exhausts have been publicly scrutinized. Shoppers blew the whistle, and with a fire under their butts, the food, architecture, and car industries made huge shifts. Local and global standards have shifted and yet the fashion industry lags light-years behind. Why is that?

SHIFT is key. A shift in shopping behavior creates a shift in fabric buying, which shifts how things are grown, which can shift the health of the people working hard to make your T-shirt; hence **#MakeShiftHappen.** While many activists take to only pointing out all the shitty things brands do, we have a solution-based philosophy about giving "bad kids" (the brands, in this case) gold stars when they make positive strides. Sharing the good things that a bad kid does usually triggers them to do more good, rather than more evil. Trust me, greenwashing (presenting something in a misleading way in order to make it seem environmentally-friendly) is a sneaky thing to do. It's deceitful and manipulative. However, one small, healthy shift made by a big brand can have a lot of impact. It's important to call out the bad shit while also acknowledging positive steps taken.

TRANSPARENCY is key. Read a brand's "About" page. It's about damn time we expected more from brands. We have the right to question what our clothes are made of. We have an opportunity and an obligation to make informed decisions. *How to Shop for Shi(f)t* will attempt to make sense of a lot of the conflicting information out there. As shoppers, we also have the right to choose what works for us as individuals, just like choosing what we want to eat. Like fast food, fast fashion has its own bodily repercussions from instant gratification.

TARYN HIPWELL

Founder of Beyond the Label

A question is often posed when a charitable organization launches: **"What happened that triggered the founder to address the issue?"** To that, I present a timeline of all my fashion-related physical issues. I am a self-declared litmus test for everything that sucks in the fabric industry.

Age: 5
Ailment: Itchy skin
Causes: Detergent and toxic chemicals
I was allergic to all detergents except for Tide. Somehow my body decided it was the least toxic of all the brands (not-so-fun fact: toxic detergents also trigger yeast infections).

Age: 10
Ailment: Rash
Causes: Finishing chemicals, fire retardant spray, formaldehyde
My grandma would buy school clothes for myself and my sisters, who were able to wear the clothes that they picked straight out of the Kmart in Cranberry, Twp., PA, while I had to wait a week for my mom to wash mine so it wouldn't irritate my skin.

Age: 16
Ailment: Eczema
Causes: Fragrance (from clothing and beauty products)
In high school, I had eczema breakouts on my eyelids and the backs of my arms, due to the fragrances used in fabric softeners, eyeshadow, makeup, body washes, and lotions.

Age: 22
Ailment: Nausea and hives
Causes: Fabrics, dyes, off-gassing from dyes, fur, and formaldehyde
When I was hired to my dream job in New York City right out of college for a high-end fashion brand, I became nauseous from fabric dyes off-gassing (when a chemical in the clothing is released in the form of an often toxic gas) and broke out in hives on my forearms from cutting purple mohair fur that had been sprayed with formaldehyde to keep the fur from decomposing.

Age: 24
Ailment: Welts
Causes: Fur and formaldehyde
Once while working at a high-end boutique in Upper East Side, Manhattan, I was carrying a rabbit fur sweater up from the stockroom, holding it against my chest. By the time I hit the storeroom floor, my skin had turned purple and broken out in welts.

Age: 35
Ailment: Mini-migraine
Causes: Off-gassing dyes and petroleum-based stretch polyester
While at Comic-Con, I almost bought a $5 pair of black leggings at CVS. Instinctively, I smelled them, and put them back because they reeked of gasoline (some synthetic fabrics are a byproduct of the petroleum industry).

Age: 38
Ailment: Nausea, migraine, and green in the face
Causes: Off-gassing dyes and petroleum-based faux leather
I walked into an Old Navy in Florida to purchase basics for my niece's school uniform, and almost immediately got a migraine from the chemical off-gassing as soon as the doors opened.

Age: 40
Ailment: Leaky armpits
Causes: Polyester and petroleum
My body had conveniently decided it wouldn't tolerate any more synthetics when I was at a posh Hollywood party wearing a beautiful dress lined with polyester. My elbows suddenly started dripping from perspiration and it was then and there that I realized polyester literally makes my armpits leak.

I'm aware that most people will never experience the specific issues that I've outlined above, yet I still wonder: if all of these chemicals are harming me, what are they doing to you? And how are the makers of these clothing items affected – the workers who have to come in direct contact with toxic fabric chemicals as part of their job? I'm also curious how most people don't have any point of reference to connect fabric chemicals to cancer. As shoppers, our desire for self-expression through fashion shouldn't come at the cost of our personal well-being or that of the people who make our clothes.

Janelle Hipwell Photography

The City of Santa Monica's Office of Sustainability and the Environment and **Sustainable Works** in conjunction with **Beyond the Label** launched the **2nd Annual Beyond the Label Sustainable Fashion Show & Tell**! The BtL team celebrating a successful sold out event and proudly wearing LA Relaxed BtL nutrition label tees made with recycled cotton from Recover Textiles. Taryn is supporting the fabulous SITA Couture in a sassy, sustainable, spa-tastic mini.

Environmental Scientist and Founder of Sustainable Daisy fashion blog

I grew up wearing jelly bracelets, Hello Kitty T-shirts, and rainbow sneakers. There wasn't much to do in my hometown of Corona, California, so my friends and I would save up $20 or so, head to our mall's Forever 21, and go wild – because we could buy one, two, maybe even three clothing items for that price (don't even get me started on the accessories). It was a fleeting pleasure that usually lasted a couple of hours, but then I would stuff it all into a drawer of other clothes I didn't really need.

This wasn't my only trashy behavior. I used to sand down brand new Converse sneakers to look beat up – the 2000s were a weird time, fashion-wise – and I bought T-shirts in my school's colors to splatter paint on them for a football game, only to throw them away a few days later. Relatable, anyone?

It wasn't until I grew up and a little wiser, that I realized this pretty facade of fashion is a mask hiding the reality of something much more sinister and ugly. I realized it was actually *me* who was the problem. I mean, I didn't think I was a criminal for wanting to buy new clothes. The stores are fun and colorful, and the music beckons me inside, making me want to dance and shop.

Consumerism was a way of life for me. But one thing I have known deep in my heart for a long time is that I wanted to make a positive impact in the world.

I studied environmental science and went to work for the California EPA as an environmental scientist. I started a sustainable fashion blog, recycled everything that left my apartment, and banished single-use plasticware. As a scientist, hazmat specialist, and a lover of life, I can attest to the fact that protecting the planet feels good, and fashion is a great place to start.

Eco Fashion Advocate

Growing up in Michigan, I loved the outdoors. I also happened to love clothing. For a long time, I thought of these as opposing interests. Nature, to me, was a constant beauty and force that was always there, but fashion was dynamic — an industry that was always changing and where things were being created.

For example, as a kid, I loved anything found in the neon palette — colors not found in nature. I preferred to dress in neon-colored sweatsuits that I would coordinate with intentionally mismatched socks. I wasn't afraid of bold choices (clearly) and I was picky about what I wore.

In high school, I discovered fashion magazines and saw that there was a whole world of options out there that were larger than my rural surroundings. I ended up going to college for business, because that was the responsible thing to do, but as soon as I finished, I threw myself into the fashion world. I was lucky enough to work both for magazines and designers I had grown up idolizing. And while I loved it, I also quickly discovered the not-so-pretty side to the industry. These expensive and beautiful garments were often not made in a beautiful way. I saw the dark side — the unregulated chemical dumping in developing nations, horrific treatment of workers, and a machine-like fashion system that would churn out more pieces than the world could ever consume, creating obscene amounts of waste and pollution in the process.

Once I became aware of all this, I knew I needed to focus my energy and efforts on making it better. I realized that nature and fashion are not opposites. They are, in fact, closely related, but the beauty of nature will not always be there if the beauty of fashion is created irresponsibly.

CHAPTER 2:

Where'd You Get That?
*Types of **Shopping Habits** & How to Shop With Intention*

We're often asked **"What to look for?"** and **"Where to find it?"** when it comes to healthier, cleaner, more sustainable fashion. We believe this depends on your shopping habits and personal style.

People shop in different ways, so where do you fall in?

- **Amazon Prime Enthusiasts:** Hunts for affordable and unique items on Amazon.com and loves Amazon Prime for next day delivery.

- **Bargain Hunters:** Fiends for the thrill of the hunt to find the best product at the lowest price.

- **Blog Stalkers:** Researches blogs before shopping for anything.

- **E-Shoppers:** Scours online e-commerce clothing websites for fashion finds.

- **Impulse Buyers:** Buys items on a whim, oftentimes with no rhyme or reason.

- **Label Lovers:** We've decided to toss the concept of brand-loving "label whores" (a general term thrown around in the fashion industry) and invented a care label-loving Label Lover. We recommend reading a care label before the brand label. Your skin is your largest organ and it will love you for it.

- **Mall Fashionistas:** Shops primarily at big-box stores, chain stores, and quite possibly, fast fashion stores.

- **Souvenir Sisters:** Seeks gifts for friends, family, and memories.

- **Vegan Vixens:** Shops animal-free, cruelty-free, leather, fur, and silk-free.

Shopping criteria to look for:

*We want to make sustainable shopping easy! In a perfect world, all brands would check off on all the below criteria, but for this guidebook, we've created a **"What to look for?"** short list, per shopping habit.*

- **Clean Production:** Healthy production standards in every stage in the making of a garment (supply chain)

- **Chemical-Free:** No harsh or polluting ingredients used in the making of the fabric or item of clothing

- **Ethical Labor:** People being treated kindly and compensated fairly for their work

- **Local Production:** Clothing produced within an approximate 100 mile radius

- **Local Sourcing**: Ingredients sourced within in an approximate 100 mile radius

- **Organic Fabrics:** Fabric that's free of toxic pesticides

- **Recycled Fabric:** Virgin fabric made from resources that are considered waste

- **Recycled Fashion:** Clothes chopped up and made into new garments

- **Sustainable Fabric:** Fabric that takes people, planet, and profit into consideration

- **Upcycled:** Converting waste into a more valuable item – trash to treasure!

- **Zero Waste:** No waste created in the production process and no packaging

HOLIDAY FEAST

HOW TO NAVIGATE
THE BUSIEST SHOPPING TIME OF THE YEAR, EVERY YEAR

Black Friday (in stores and online)

- Go hiking instead!

- If you do go to a mall, **BUY ONLY WHAT YOU NEED**, not just what's on sale.

- Look for brands with clearly labeled organic and recycled fabric. They are out there!

Small Business Saturday (in stores and online)

- Support the SBA (Small Business Administration) by purchasing from local businesses that are transparent about their methods, source locally, and use sustainable fabrics.

Sustainable Sundays (in stores and online)

- Let's get this eco, ethos, and ethics party started! Support businesses that are transparent and use sustainable fabrics.

Cyber Monday (online)

- Support online businesses big, small, local, or global that are transparent and use sustainable fabrics.

Giving Tuesday (in stores and online)

- Transparency is key. If a brand claims to be donating a portion of their proceeds to a worthy cause, still take the extra step and do your homework to make sure they care about people and the planet throughout their supply chain.

1. Amazon Prime Enthusiasts

These days, shopping from the comfort of your own home has never been more convenient. This shopper prefers to hunt for affordable, unique items online in one marketplace, and loves the next day delivery that Amazon Prime affords them.

WHAT TO LOOK FOR:

ORGANIC FABRICS ⟳ RECYCLED MATERIALS ⟳ ETHICAL LABOR

BRAIN CANDY

Read through the product reviews to see how authentic and transparent a brand really is. Shoppers are smart, and will often do their own research to verify what a brand is telling them or claiming to be. Just like using Yelp to steer you to a tasty meal, let other shoppers' opinions guide you to the good stuff.

Our suggestion is to stick to organic basics when you're first starting to shop for clothes online. Remember though: one sustainable offering from a brand doesn't mean the rest of the line isn't toxic and conventionally produced – do your homework.

Better basics are easy to find on Amazon:

⟳ Organic socks

⟳ Organic underwear

⟳ Organic T-shirts

TASTY TREAT:

See what comes up when you search "organic T-shirts," "sustainable clothing," "eco-friendly fashion," or "recycled jewelry" on Amazon.

Fun Finds:

- Earrings made of recycled metal rulers, bottle caps, and bike parts

- Bracelets made of recycled flip-flops

- Wallets made of recycled inner tubes

2. *Bargain Hunters*

Do you thrive on the thrill of the hunt, or shrill after finding the best product at the lowest price? Bargain Hunters pride themselves on getting good deals and sniffing out sales. Many are secondhand shoppers who love rummaging through racks to find a special gem.

WHAT TO LOOK FOR:

ORGANIC FABRICS   ○   UPCYCLED   ○   RECYCLED FASHION

BRAIN CANDY

Have you ever met a professional bargain hunter? We're not talking about someone who brags about getting a $15 pair of jeans at an outlet mall (which is not f'n cool, by the way!). We're talking about a stylist who gets paid to scour estate sales, resale shops, vintage stores, consignment shops, thrift stores, and flea markets for incredible clothing.

Unfortunately, outlet malls support a broken system of overproduction, in which the creation of clothing to be sold in a store is more than the demand for the location. Meanwhile, resale shops are doing their best to reduce mass amounts of clothing waste. On average, only 13% of clothes donated to thrift shops are ever sold in stores. So where does the other 87% go? The export of secondhand clothes to developing countries used to be a viable business, but that's not the case not anymore. The clothes are sorted by quality, then some clothes are re-sold in stores and at markets – some made into rags, some incinerated, while other pile up in the landfills outside of the U.S. Country by country, Africa is refusing to continue being a fast fashion landfill for the U.S. and Europe alike. Rwanda, Kenya, and Tanzania are each in the process of banning secondhand clothing altogether in order to boost their own domestic clothing production.

When you shop secondhand, you're not only helping to reduce waste. You're also reducing the use of chemicals, water, and resources needed to make virgin fabric for clothing. Give your purchases purpose!

> **"Shopping secondhand** highlights the value of what's well-made and has a **story behind it**. For example, finding a beautiful, vintage skirt from a French consignment shop filled me with a special feeling that no department store could ever replicate. Thrifted clothes are **artifacts** of the **stylish person who wore it before you."**
>
> – Karen Housel, environmental scientist and founder of Sustainable Daisy fashion blog

Los Angeles' Top Resale Shops:

- American Cancer Society Discovery Shop
- Buffalo Exchange
- Closet Trading Company
- The Colleagues
- Crossroads Trading Co.
- Out of the Closet

- It's a Wrap!
- Goodwill
- Salvation Army
- Wasteland
- Plato's Closet
- Jet Rag*

Yay! Jet Rag's $1 Sunday is one of LA's best-kept secrets. You can buy slightly damaged and typically tossed items that don't make it into the store for $1.

Yay! Find a thrift store in your city. TheThriftShopper.com

Online Thrifting & Apps:

- **eBay:** An auction-style website where people buy and sell fashion apparel and other items

- **Etsy:** A global marketplace of handmade, vintage, and creative goods (Remember: not all goods are good! Look out for good quality, sustainable fabrics, and ethically-made items).

- **Depop:** An e-commerce app for creatives to sell funky fashion finds

- **Mercari:** A fashion app that is a hassle-free and secure way for anyone to buy and sell stuff straight from their mobile device

- **Poshmark:** A fashion app, which is the largest social marketplace for fashion where people from the U.S. can buy, sell, and share their style with others

- **Material World:** A subscription-based personalized secondhand designer box that shoppers order online to be sent to their doorstep

- **Swap Society:** A virtual clothing exchange website where there's no buying or selling — only swapping! Refresh your wardrobe without shopping, with unlimited swapping and free shipping both ways.

- **RealReal:** The leader in authenicated luxury consignment (100% real)

- **thredUP:** A fashion resale website for consumers to buy and sell secondhand clothing online

- **Tradesy:** A website that makes resale fast, simple, and stylish — for buyers and sellers alike

Yay! thredUP is also part of a larger "collaborative consumption" movement, which encourages shoppers to embrace the sharing economy.

Yay! National Consignment Day is October 1st.

3. Blog Stalkers

Before shopping for anything, do you find yourself researching online and obsessively tapping into your favorite blogger's Instagrams for their style credits? No matter what it is you're in need of — be it a zero waste jacket, organic undies, or vegan shoes — there's a blogger out there that can help you weed through the noise and point you in the right direction. We, here at Beyond the Label started blogging to connect with fellow sustainable fashion junkies. So trust us when we tell you that they exist - and they're rad! Just check out our Instagram followers. They are leaders from around the world that #MakeShiftHappen on a regular basis. We 💜 you!

WHAT TO LOOK FOR:

LOCAL PRODUCTION   ↻   ETHICAL LABOR   ↻   ZERO WASTE

BRAIN CANDY

Don't be shy! Reach out to bloggers via direct message or respond to their posts. Ask questions. Make some virtual friends. Most likely, someone else is also looking for a red, organic hemp beanie with mustard-colored tassels. Don't be afraid to harness the power of social media and crowdsource an answer.

> **"***I love eco fashion lines and eco fashion blogs, and I look forward to a **future** when we won't need to say "eco" any longer, because all fashion lines will be created in **eco conscious** and **cruelty-free** ways. A big shoutout to the brands and blogs that are paving the way for this conscious **movement** to go mainstream.***"**
>
> *— Nicholas J. Brown, eco fashion advocate*

TASTY TREAT:

There are tons of eco and fashion bloggers out there! If you want to keep up with trends without having to log hours of research yourself, start by following a couple from our list of favorites. Let their passion and expertise inspire you to shop with intention.

Bloggers:

- **Agnes Muljadi, *Artsy Agnes*** - A passionate vegan ballerina

- **Alden Wicker, *EcoCult*** - An unapologetic, sustainably-minded New Yorker

- **Allison Sherman, *Allison Carol*** - An adventurous vegan/eco fashion, travel, and lifestyle blog

- **AmyAnn & Blake Cadwell, *The Good Trade*** - A dedicated social good publication

- **Andrea Plell, *Ecologique Fashion*** - A co-founder of the Sustainable Fashion Alliance

- **Elizabeth Stilwell, *The Note Passer*** - An inspirational source of information about waste reduction

- **Faye Lessler, *Sustaining Life*** - A leading sustainability educator and role model

- **Jennifer Nini, *Eco Warrior Princess*** - An empowering green living influencer

- **Joshua Katcher, *A Discerning Brute*** - An influential men's fashion, food, and etiquette space

- **Kamea Chayne, *Conscious Fashion Collective*** - A collective inspiring a sustainable fashion journey

- **Karen Housel, *Sustainable Daisy*** - A colorful, eco-friendly lifestyle influencer

- **Katie Pruett, *Ethical Style Journal*** - A new kind of fashion magazine. In digital and print

- **Katie Roberts, *Sustainability in Style*** - A sustainable platform committed to mindful consciousness

- **Kelly Sheenan, *Peppermint Magazine*** - A print magazine available across Australia, internationally and online

- ***Laura Engelke, The Sustainable Stylist*** - A leading stylist that guides followers to sustainable brands

- **Lauren Singer, *Trash for Tossers*** - A how-to blog for a cost-effective, zero waste lifestyle blog

- **Leah Wise, *Style Wise*** - A conscious consumer and social justice advocate

- **Magaly Fuentez, *Eco Fashion Week*** (EFW) - An empowering blog and series of fashions show that are not to be missed in Vancouver and Seattle

- **Melissa Wong, *House of Gratia et Caritas*** - Lists charitable organizations that give back fashionably

- **Natalie Kay, *Sustainably Chic*** - A responsible, sustainable fashion blog

- **Renee Peters, *Model 4 Green Living*** - Practical tips for mindful living

- **Rhian HY, *WifeLife*** - A tatted fab beauty expert wife that has been known to put out great videos about sustainable fashion

- **Summer Edwards, *Tortoise and Lady Grey*** - A slow-fashion lifestyle blog

- **Taryn Hipwell and BtL Team, *LA Beyond the Label*** - A science-based, sustainable fashion platform

Yay! Special shoutouts to some of our Instgram followers and peeps we are following: CallMeNaomiG, EthicalWriters, FairFashionOOTD, GlobalFashionExchange, TheFashionLaw, ConsciousNChic, EnglishLassInLA, ChristenGerhart, VeganScene, SustainablyStylish, SustainYourStyle, StylesForThought, and HolisticHaley.

4. E-Shoppers

Do you scour e-commerce clothing sites for fashion finds and despise frequenting the mall? Do you prefer shopping while sitting in bed in your pajamas? It's convenient, we get it!

WHAT TO LOOK FOR:

LOCAL PRODUCTION ○ CLEAN PRODUCTION METHODS ○ SUSTAINABLE FABRICS

BRAIN CANDY

When shopping online, go straight to the "About" page. Read each brand's mission and vision statements so you can feel confident about where you're putting your money. Look for sites that your favorite eco fashion bloggers refer to as well.

> **"Online shopping** comes with a lot of perks – you can do it at any time of the day, you can search for exactly what you want, and you can try things on in the comfort of your own home. But online shopping also presents its own **unique challenges**. I always recommend starting by looking at three things: **country of origin, fabric content,** and **size chart** – these will give you a lot of information about the garment. I also always recommend you read the company's 'About' page to get a sense of who they are. Look for specifics! Words like "eco-friendly" and "sustainable" aren't quite specific enough, however terms like **"organic"** or **"fair trade"** are more substantive. Some of my favorite resources to find ethical brands online are Fair Trade LA, and, of course, Bead & Reel.**"**
>
> – Sica Schmitz, founder of online activist fashion shop Bead & Reel

TASTY TREAT:

Online shopping websites that vet the brands they sell:

- **Bead & Reel:** All the offerings are vegan and sweatshop-free, with an emphasis on female-founded and eco-friendly brands
- **Enrou:** Sells jewelry, accessories, and socially conscious home goods, all of which empower the lives of the people who make them
- **MooShoes:** Sells shoes and other vegan accessories that are cruelty-free and animal-approved
- **Modavanti:** Fashion and beauty items that prioritize sustainable production – good for you, good for others, and good for the earth!

5. Impulse Buyers

If you've been known to buy items on a whim, often when there's no rhyme or reason or real occasion, this is probably you (sometimes we call this "Sparkly Pretty Thing Syndrome"). Never fear, we have fun brain games for you!

WHAT TO LOOK FOR:

ETHICAL LABOR   ↻   SUSTAINABLE FABRICS   ↻   ORGANIC FABRICS

BRAIN CANDY

Walmart and many mall stores engineer their shopping experience so that shoppers are enticed by sale items and low-prices. Our brains find it hard to resist!

Instead of berating yourself, acknowledge the struggle and find ways to resist the impulse by playing some quick mind games with yourself, like this one below:

TASTY TREAT:

Before buying something impulsively, run through this 30-second mental checklist:

- Do I really *need* this?

- Do I even *like* this?

- Will I *wear* this 30 times or more?

If you do come to the conclusion: "I really do need new super soft underwear!" or "My winter coat smells like cat urine and the smell just won't wash out!" or "I need to look smart and savvy at my new job," shelve the guilt and SHOP AWAY! It feels great to adjust your spending habits.

6. Label Lovers

Choosing pieces by evaluating them on their "eco, ethos, and ethics" is important! This one's for our intentional shoppers who take the time to read a care label before blindly following and buying from a brand.

WHAT TO LOOK FOR:

ETHICAL LABOR   ○   CLEAN PRODUCTION METHODS   ○   SUSTAINABLE FABRICS

BRAIN CANDY

Just because a brand is expensive, and considered "luxury," it doesn't mean that the money spent covers livable wages for its makers or ensures that the production process is clean and sustainable. A decade ago, eco fashion pioneer Linda Loudermilk posed the question, "What is luxury?" to the fashion industry and shoppers alike. Consider this: Luxury is the ability to spend expendable money on desired items, while keeping every single person in the supply chain in mind. We call this the mindful luxury movement.

It's easier to imagine that only fast fashion is responsible for the evils of the industry, but that isn't the case. Each of us has the opportunity and ability to make the lives of workers in the garments industry healthier, and – dare we say – more enjoyable, through the power of shopping.

TASTY TREAT:

Kering, a global luxury group, has committed to crafting more sustainable luxury by 2025, and we're excited to see what they will unveil over the next few years! Here are a few brands under Kering's umbrella that we'll have our eye on:

- **Gucci:** A leading fashion house, has announced that it is going fur-free, as the material is no longer modern

- **Stella McCartney:** A high-end fashion designer and activewear designer that does not use leather, skins, fur, or feathers in any of their products, and is investing in and using new innovative fabric technologies

- **Puma:** An activewear company that is bluesign certified — meaning they use sustainable ingredients, clean processing, and safely manufactured products

Yay! C&A, an international chain of fashion retail clothing stores, is focused on *Making Sustainable Fashion the New Normal*. BtL is newly introduced to their efforts and we are curious to understand their affordable pricing. #WearTheChange Cradle to Cradle Certified Gold denim.

7. Mall Fashionistas

Do you live in an area where malls and mini-malls still reign supreme? If so, you probably shop primarily at big-box and chain stores, and your closet has its fair share of fast fashion. Eco-friendly fashion is likely hard to come by in your neck of the woods, but there are still ways to improve your shopping habits.

WHAT TO LOOK FOR:

ORGANIC FABRICS ◌ RECYCLED FABRICS ◌ RECYCLED CLOTHING

Yay! Urban Outfitters and H&M sell clothes made from recycled secondhand clothing. Boo-yah!

BRAIN CANDY

There are multiple fast fashion brands that are being exposed publicly for unethical and environmentally unsafe practices. Malls contain many clothing options that provide shoppers with "throw away fashion" – clothes made to fit the trend today and can be tossed when the trend changes tomorrow. Currently trend change is fluid and seasonal. Andrew Morgan, director and producer of The True Cost documentary, made a huge splash in 2015 when his film exposed the evils of fast fashion and the unethical treatment of garment workers. As unsettling as Morgan's film was, the positive result was that it caused millions of people who watched it to question their fashion choices and consider shifting their shopping habits, which in turn shifted brands to become more mindful, in order to keep customers.

But let's take a minute to compare fast fashion giants H&M and Forever 21. Both create clothes with controlled obsolescence in mind, meaning clothing made to break or be disposed of in a short amount of time without losing brand loyalty. But only H&M has an extensive sustainability fashion grant program that surpasses what could be considered greenwashing. While this doesn't excuse all the evils of polluting habits they may still engage in, at least they're making strides and positive steps forward. H&M's Global Change Award grant is an innovation challenge seeking game-changing ideas that can help make the fashion industry more circular.

Yay! We appreciate actresses like Olivia Wilde, Emma Watson, and Amber Valletta for choosing to wear sustainability-minded options like H&M's Conscious Collection on the red carpet to educate shoppers about sustainable fashion and fabric choices.

> *"We are seeing some dramatic commitments from H&M and European retailer C&A that will cause a **fundamental shift** in the demand for **sustainable cotton** and other **sustainable recycled fibers**. All it takes are a few large companies to begin this systemic change towards more sustainable fibers to eliminate millions of tons of pesticides and **save millions** of yards of fabric from landfills."*
>
> *– Jason Kibbey, CEO of Sustainable Apparel Coalition*

Yay! Clothing brands Patagonia and Eileen Fisher are committed to transparency and encourage other brands to learn from their innovative, recycled, and sustainable fabrics, dyes, and production processes.

TASTY TREAT:

These retailers receive honorable mentions for offering sustainable options at select locations. Let's get more shift happening in stores!

Retailers:

- **Adidas:** ASK FOR hemp T-shirts, coconut fiber jackets, certified leather and ocean plastic fabric shoes.
- **Aldo:** ASK FOR shoes Certified by the Leather Working Group and ASK what does the certification mean?
- **Anthropologie:** ASK FOR more Lacausa (LA-CA-USA), Boyish, and Mara Hoffman
- **Athleta:** ASK FOR organic cotton shorts and pants, and their recycled polyester stretch options.
- **H&M:** ASK FOR the Conscious Collections (made with organic cotton and TENCEL™, a sustainable fabric) and Close the Loop recycled clothing line.
- **Levi's:** ASK FOR recycled fiber, vintage, or "low-water" denim.
- **Nordstrom:** ASK FOR brands like The North Face, Patagonia, Eileen Fisher, Timberland, and Stella McCartney.
- **Primark** (Europe and U.S. Yay!): ASK ABOUT ethical standards, certifications on fabrics.
- **Target:** ASK FOR sustainable cotton. That is all! One huge upgrade.
- **Urban Outfitters:** ASK FOR the Urban Renewal recycled clothing line. And if they don't offer it, request it.
- **Zara:** ASK FOR their vegan options.

Yay! It's really exciting to hear that Target is committed to 100% sustainable cotton by 2022.

Yay! Zara is working with PETA to find leather options that don't require animals.

8. *Souvenir Sisters*

Do you love grabbing gifts for friends, family, and even yourself when you're on vacation? If so, you're probably no stranger to hotel gift shops and you've already scouted where the popular souvenir stops are on your trip. Memorabilia is a huge market, and there's nothing wrong with snagging a souvenir as a physical keepsake.

WHAT TO LOOK FOR:

LOCAL PRODUCTION ○ ETHICAL LABOR ○ UPCYCLED

BRAIN CANDY

For the most part, cruises and tourist attractions sell cheap, toxic, and unethically-made clothing to turn a quick profit. In reality, the "2 T-shirts for $20" so-called deal is a way for a cruise line to encourage guests to leave with a branded takeaway to promote the company long after they've disembarked. Instead, consider hopping off the ship and shopping from local artisans and craftspeople, which will legitimately support the local community and economy. ***If you know you are going somewhere that may sell unique pieces, reach out to the designer to see if you can stop by.***

TASTY TREAT:

Sites that support brands worth visiting:

Hand-crafted items are available for purchase online for couch travelers: (people who travel to foreign lands through their computer or TV).

- The Peace Exchange // Enrou // Ten Thousand Villages
- Indigenous and ORG by vio work with indigenous tribes.

---

*"I used to have a **love/hate relationship** with **souvenir shopping** while on vacation. It made me uncomfortable because I couldn't do research before shopping, and cheap gift store clothes typically smell horrid to me, so I'd get frustrated. Now part of my vacations typically includes meeting **local designers**. The next time I make it to Haiti, I'm so looking forward to going to **Ten Thousand Villages,** which **supports Haitian artists** by purchasing the **hand-crafted items** they create (usually natural or recycled) using time-honored skills."*

– Taryn Hipwell, founder of Beyond the Label

9. Vegan Vixens

First, let's get a few things straight:

Vegan Clothing is any garment made without animal products — as in no leather, suede, fur, or even silk — because murdering a silkworm is still harming an animal! Read on if you're interested in making your closet an animal-free zone.

WHAT TO LOOK FOR:

LOCAL PRODUCTION ⟳ ETHICAL SOURCING ⟳ RECYCLED CLOTHING

BRAIN CANDY

You may not have the stamina to eat vegan, but vegan fashion is important because it, among other things, reduces toxic chemicals from neighboring water systems. The less animal-based products you buy, the more you'll help out our furry or water friends.

Yay! Thank you Stella McCartney for being a pioneer in fur-free fashion.

Yay! PETA and Sustainable Source Studios are connecting large brands with fabulous sustainable and fur-free fabric replacements.

TASTY TREAT:

SUSI's **"The Miley" Black Gingham Platforms** as worn by Miss Cyrus at the Ariana Grande's "One Love Manchester" benefit for the **We Love Manchester Emergency Fund**

*"Fashion is more than the clothes we wear: It's the story we tell the world about who we are. **Animal skins** are loaded with **toxic chemicals** like arsenic and formaldehyde to keep them from decomposing, which is why the majority of brands like Free People, Gap Inc., Topshop and Zara have incorporated plenty of vegan styles into their collections – everything from vegan leather strappy sandals and jackets to microfiber cross-body purses to straw boater or **faux suede** hats. Some higher-end vegan fashion houses include Brave GentleMan, NICORA Shoes, SUSI Studio, and VAUTE, which offers fashion composed of **pineapple-leaf 'leather,' cork, polyurethane** constructed from **recycled plastic** bottles, and **post-industrial polyester**. Leading fabric manufacturers in this arena include Majilite, Piñatex, and Ultrasuede for **vegan leather,** and PrimaLoft and Thinsulate for down alternatives. Wool-free blends made of **acrylic, bamboo, cotton, hemp, TENCEL™**, and **viscose** are also available. With all of today's options, it's never been easier to look killer without killing animals or the environment."*

– Christina Sewell, senior fashion campaigner and campaigns division at PETA

━━━━━━━━━ **Food for thought:** ━━━━━━━━━

How would your closet shift if you chose clothing that was both beautiful and cruelty-free?

CHAPTER 3:

What Shall I Wear Today?
Types of Personal Style & Which Brands Fit Your Look

Is it possible to **embrace sustainable fashion** without compromising your **style** or your **budget?** We'll offer up some creative, affordable ways to look great and align yourself with your **values.**

Which style category best describes your personal fashion sense?

If we missed a type of style that you wear, like Soccer Mom, Cosplay or Harujuku Doll, reach out to us at LABeyondtheLabel.com. We love to share new brands, styles, and innovations on Instagram and Facebook **(@labeyondthelabel)** to keep everyone up to date.

1. **Boho Chic**

2. **Bootcamp**

3. **Clubgoer**

4. **The F'n Boss**

5. **Hipster**

6. **Jeans & T-Shirt**

7. **Prom & Red Carpet**

8. **Rocker Chic**

9. **Skater/Surfer**

10. **Sunday Brunch**

11. **Yogi All Day**

In this chapter, we'll be recommending one T-shirt per style category, so you can get a feel for what product information to pay attention to. There are a plethora of healthy fashion options out there for any personal style!

The T-shirts found while writing the book may change, but we're confident there will be a similar item offered by the brand.

If you have a favorite T-shirt brand that we missed, let us know "What's in your tee?" at #WhatsInYourTee

1. Boho Chic

From summer music festivals to springtime happy hours, you can't go wrong with a floor-grazing floral maxi dress. It's the perfect mixture of classy and whimsical, comfy and flowy. It packs easy for traveling and, for our festival goers out there, it's a Coachella must-have!

STAPLES:

- Maxi dresses

- Peasant tops

- Denim shirts and jackets

- Pair with sandals, flats, wedges, and cowboy boots

Buy new: People Tree, Poeme, Reformation, Bead & Reel, Christy Dawn, Abask, Yireh, Artisan & Fox, St. Roche, Lemlem, Sage Larock, Studio One Eighty Nine

Buy used: thredUP (it has an entire "Boho Style" section!), vintage Levi's shorts and jackets

Yay! To find local resale shops near you, check out the online resource TheThriftShopper.com. Or check out the L.A.'s Top Resale Shops list under Bargain Hunters in Chapter 2.

DIY: Add fringe to a denim jacket. Consider using vintage scarves as tops

Accessories: ORG by vio, Fahmina, Dimmblá, Beau Monde Organics, The Tote Project

———— WHAT TEE look FOR! ————

Yay! PACT Women's V-Neck, $15.99
Yay! Studio One Eighty Nine was Co-founded by Abrima Erwiah and Rosario Dawson (also a HUGE Celeb Crush). We do have a crush on Rosario Dawson, and this deserves a Yay! as well. Pricepoint reflects craftsmanship. Shoes under $150.

Celeb Crush: Anne Hathaway, the ultimate bohemian princess, pulls off the most beautiful thrift finds at farmers markets and on red carpets. We love her for boasting about her $15 flea market find on Good Morning America during the press tour for her film Colossal.

DEEP FRIED THOUGHTS

Every year, brands churn out collections specifically for music festival season – Coachella in particular. But whether you're heading to Indio or not, you can still enjoy the fashion. Consider a fair trade find as opposed to something cheap and tossable. When you choose to shop fairly, each purchase you make is an investment in someone else's future.

2. Bootcamp

No-nonsense, self-motivated, and goal-oriented. This tough cookie is on a mission. Clothing needs to fit well with no fuss for this multitasking, marathon running, trailblazer who gets shit done.

STAPLES:

- T-shirts

- Body-hugging shorts and leggings

- Tank tops

- Sports bras

Buy new: Boody, prAna, Patagonia, Blue Canoe, Threads for Thought

Buy used: Due to the sweaty body factor, we prefer to purchase new for most items. However, outerwear, like hoodies and windbreakers, can be fabulous thrifty finds.

Accessories: LE BUNS (undies)

───────── WHAT TEE look FOR! ─────────

Yay! Patagonia Women's Blythewood Tee, $35

Super Yay! CHECK OUT: Patagonia's The Footprint Chronicles is an online resource that brings supply chain transparency to a new level by showing the farms, fabric mills, and sewing factories on an interactive map. You can click on the map to see specific details, like the number of workers, gender ratio, languages spoken, and which products are made in each factory.

Celeb Crush: Reese Witherspoon, who portrayed Cheryl Strayed in 2014's blockbuster Wild - a movie about a woman who hiked the grueling Pacific Crest Trail solo in order to search for clarity and closure - has been spotted wearing Patagonia while running errands!

DEEP FRIED THOUGHTS

Poly, synthetic, and spandex are all fabrics that off-gas and feed your pores nondigestible micro-fragments of plastic. Yuck!

3. Clubgoer

The party animal who lets it loose on the dance floor. A little booty shaking does a body good. Sexy used to mean push-up bras, short skirts, and long legs. These days self-expression is sexy, so dare to bare or not to bare. And if you want to wear something backless, this is the time to break it out.

STAPLES:

- ○ Form-fitting dress

- ○ Heels, hoops, or dangling earrings that go bling

- ○ Jeans, T-shirt, and shiny combat boots

- ○ Anything that makes you feel sexy

Borrow from a friend: Clubbing is always an excuse to wear whatever is in your friend's closet.

Buy new: Bella Dahl (secret formula lyocell fabric items), Arkins, People Tree, Pangean, ReMake.world, Hot as Hell

Buy used: American Rag (vintage section)

Rent online: GlamCorner (an Australian dress sharing platform)

Accessories: ElleWest, Kipato Unbranded (Kenya), Susi, Mink, Ken Wroy - men's undies (city landscapes = sassy!)

———————— WHAT TEE look FOR! ————————

Yay! Science of Apparel Non-Binary Galileo Tee, $48

Celeb Crush: Jade Chynoweth, who we adore for sporting some of the most awesome chopped up DIY cropped tops! Her dancing is off the chain and the charts, too! Go girl!

DEEP FRIED THOUGHTS

Depending on where you live, climate may dictate what is worn. In Miami the goal might be to wear as little as possible, like a bright, bold, stretchy tank dress that functions like a bathing suit due to the humidity. In L.A., it could be a classy halter dress that's cut high to show off all the hiking. In New York City, a unique shade of black dress that hugs all the right curves with a zipper from bottom to top that stops traffic. Whatever your dress choice, consider choosing fabrics that function for your need as well as your health.

4. The F'n Boss

A powerful, confident leader who empowers those around them and isn't afraid to climb the ladder, corporate or otherwise. A career-driven individual that demands excellence and integrity. #GoalDigger

STAPLES:

- Power suits in navy, red, black, or whatever color that makes you feel boss

- Structured dresses, pencil skirts, and bags

- Thin blazers

- Collared shirts

Borrow from a friend: Reach out to your aunts, mentors, and fellow bosses to see if they have anything they no longer wear

Buy new: Bead & Reel, Indigenous Clothing, Wallis Evera, Eileen Fisher, Echo & Air, Tribe Alive, Vetta, Symbology, 19th Ammendment, Authur & Henry (men's shirts), Siizu, Kestan, Faircloth + Supply, Study NY, Knowledge Cotton Apparel, the Cosmos Studio capsule collection, Mara Hoffman

Buy used: Closet Trading Company, The Colleagues, Wasteland, Goldmine Vintage

Accessories: Oka-B wedge, Matt & Nat, Shop Suspiro, Veerah, Osenhaus, Susi

Yay! Vetta - Capsule Collection 5 pieces - 30 looks. Spend a little more, SAVE A LOT!
Yay! Dress for Success supplies women in need with professional wardrobes for job interviews and so much more.

WHAT TEE look FOR!

Yay! Groceries Apparel Men's Contrast Poc Crew T-shirt, $44

Celeb Crush: Jessica Alba for being a real life f'n Boss and overall Wonder Woman for creating The Honest Company, which offers healthy home, body, and cosmetic products for young mothers and women everywhere!

DEEP FRIED THOUGHTS

Watch *The Story of Stuff* on YouTube to learn how controlled obsolescence causes shoppers to feel depressed, so that they use retail therapy to feel good again. It's a vicious cycle.

5. Hipster

It's the girl in the most hip coffee shop in an up-and-coming part of town. She's always a step ahead of the trends and has an air of mystery about her. She treats thrifting for secondhand treasures like a sport, and has an admirably eclectic sense of style.

STAPLES:

- Funky, quirky jackets and vests

- Flannel button-up shirts

- Cutoff denim shorts

- Lace-up boots

Borrow from a friend: Rifle through your grandparents' closets, if they'll let you!

Buy new: Groceries Apparel, Apolis, Fanmail, Industry of All Nations, HoodLamb, ACF, Olderbrother (gender-neutral), Mate the Label, Bleed "We bleed for nature"

Buy used: Jet Rag, American Rag Cie, Out of the Closet, Revolve Clothing Exchange (St. Pete, Fl)

Accessories: Krochet Kids, FEED, HFS Collective (Hipsters for Sisters), Allbirds, Kathumba Bag, MooShoes, Nicora, Insecta

———————— WHAT TEE look FOR! ————————

Yay! Jungmaven Stone Washed & Distressed Baja Unisex T-shirt, $55
Super Yay! Yen Zambia Founder Billy Lombe has credited BtL's Founder Taryn Hipwell for inspiring the creation of Kathumba Bags. She'd shared about reusable bags while on an Eco Fashion Education tour in Zambia. Zambia's single-use plastic waste is a huge issue and Kathumba Bags are creating awareness.
***Keep an eye out - the next run is rumored to have a quote from Taryn printed on them.**

Celeb Crush: We think Will.i.am is fantastic for everything he did to support EKO-CYCLE, which elevated the conversation about what's possible to be made out of plastic bottles (oftentimes collected at his own concerts) and everything he's doing to support innovative tech fashion and fabrics.

DEEP FRIED THOUGHTS

If you're not one for vintage clothes, there are options out there that look lived in, no harmful chemicals necessary. For example, Levi's Water<Less distressed denim utilizes an ozone process which reduces the amount of water used in comparison to regular denim production, but still makes jeans look fashionably weathered.

6. Jeans & T-shirt

This is a classic, can't-go-wrong look. With the right combination, you can pull off any assortment of looks, ranging from cute and comfortable to vintage-inspired to all-American to business casual. The possibilities are endless!

STAPLES:

- Jeans
- T-Shirt
- Heels, sneakers, boots — anything you'd like to accessorize with!

Borrow from a friend: Concert T-shirts, graphic T-shirts, even plain white T-shirts

Buy new (Jeans...see T-shirt throughout all style catagories): Kuyichi, MUD Jeans (ask about the "Lease a Jeans" program), Nudie Jeans, Triarchy, G-Star RAW, Boyish, Monkee Genes (skinny jeans and more)

Buy used: Vintage Levi's, Out of the Closet, Salvation Army

———————— WHAT TEE look FOR! ————————

Yaaaaaaaaaaay! Beyond the Label / MetaWear Nutrition Label Tee, $28

Yaaaaaaaaaaay! Beyond the Label / LA Relaxed Nutrition Label Tee, $28

Yaaaaaaaaaaay! Beyond the Label / LA Relaxed "Comical Care Label" Tee, $44

Celeb Crushes *(We have a few, so stay with us)***:**

- **T-shirt** - Moby for being a vegan restaurateur and truly appreciating the BtL tee at Green Fest LA.

- **Jeans** - The British Royal Family who are hosting sustainable fashion project. Meghan Markle's already been spotted in Triarchy denim.

- **Both** - Pharrell uses his star power to share the dangers of ocean plastics through fashion, bringing recognition to Bionic Yarn (fabric made with recycled ocean plastics), Parley for the Ocean (nonprofit), and a partnership with G-Star RAW. Dutch denim brand, G-Star RAW, is on a mission to change the fashion industry with the launch of their most sustainable denim ever, and they are gifting its technique and technology to the entire industry in a call to action (check out the article on Forbes). Change is happening and it's good for business.

DEEP FRIED THOUGHTS

Sadly, your T-shirt may have taken several resource intensive flights around the world. Cotton could be grown in Texas, fabric produced in India, fabric cut and sewn in China, and the final T-shirt distributed from Northern California around the U.S. What we're trying to say is: look for clothes that tout local production methods and sources as much as possible!

7. Prom & Red Carpet

No matter what the special occasion is – prom, the Oscars, a wedding – there are so many ways to look amazing without breaking the bank or adding extra weight to your closet. Brides-to-be, listen up: while you may want to keep your wedding dress after the big day, per tradition, your bridesmaids may not wear their dresses ever again. Try renting! And men, you've been renting tuxes for years. Go you!

STAPLES:

- ○ Prom dresses

- ○ Bridesmaid dresses

- ○ Red or "green" carpet dresses (anything from floor-length to cocktail dresses)

Borrow from a friend: Ask friends and family if they have anything on hand! You may find something unexpected.

Buy new: (pricey, yet beautiful) Vaute, Voz

Buy used: American Cancer Society Discovery Shops, The Colleagues, Cinderella's Closet U.S.A

Rent online: The Real Real, Ruby's Fashion Library, Beyond Your Wardrobe, Rent the Runway, Tux-rentals-a-plenty!

Rent on location: Albright Fashion Library (locations in both N.Y.C. and L.A.)

Accessories: Margaret Rowe, Karina Gonzalez, Cult of Coquette

---

WHAT TEE look FOR!

Yay! Eileen Fisher Micro TENCEL™ rib stitch round neck slim top T-shirt, $118

Super Yay! Check out Eileen Fisher's Behind the Label initiative, which lets shoppers peek into their clothing production process.

Celeb Crush: Props to eco fashion advocates Liv Firth and Suzy Amis for using their red carpet choices to spread the word about sustainable fashion to a global audience. Firth's Piñatex, silver pineapple fiber dress at the Met Gala, for example, (yes, she wore a red carpet dress made of shiny silver pineapple fabric). Props again to Emma Watson for utilizing the Met Gala to EDUCATE! Check out all her red, green, and gold carpet sightings at @the_press_tour on Instagram. It's brilliant.

DEEP FRIED THOUGHTS

We'd like to challenge Textile Waste Reducing Communities to come up with statistics that show how many prom dresses are biodegradable vs. non-biodegradable. How many yards of synthetic fabric would that equal per year?

8. Rocker Chic

An outspoken, fearless badass who unapologetically breaks the rules to make their own. This rebel doesn't follow the crowd and rages against the machine.

STAPLES:

- Distressed denim jeans

- Vintage leather or vegan leather jackets and boots

- Edgy, chopped-up T-shirts

- Vintage concert T-shirts

Buy new: BEETxBEET, Fokus Green, Upcycle Los Angeles

Buy used: Authentic vintage band T-shirts can be found on Etsy and eBay.

DIY: Invite friends over for a "Tee Party" to swap shirts, then grab some scissors and get creative!

Accessories: Fahmina, Chic Made Consciously (tire jewelry), MooShoes, Vinylize (sunglasses from vinyl records), NICORA

Ask for: Ask for organic tees at concerts. If the musical artist, concert venue, and T-shirt maker knows you want eco-friendly options, they'll be more inclined to make them.

— WHAT TEE look FOR! —

Yay! Commonwealth Press / Royal Apparel "Pittsburgh is Riveting" T-shirt, $25

Celeb Crush: Musicians Jack Johnson and Jason Mraz use their tour merchandise to educate shoppers about the content of their concert T-shirts. Jason Mraz partners with OrganicSound, so that he can share about zero waste by turning his obsolete concert T-shirts into new clothes! Jack Johnson has been a pioneer by using his care label area to share about the importance of organic fabrics and fair labor. We appreciate their commitment to a reduced waste, happier, and healthier fashion industry, and for setting an example for clean living!

DEEP FRIED THOUGHTS

At Beyond the Label's Upcycling Labs – held at various universities, fashion, and cultural events – we teach attendees how to upcycle organic cotton Jack Johnson concert T-shirts into reusable bags.

Yay! Jack Johnson has been kind enough to donate surplus merch to BtL for educational purposes! Nothing goes to waste.

9. Skater/Surfer

This one's for all the adventure seekers; all the movers, rollers, riders, and shakers. Whether you're in the water or skating around town, you're probably more exposed to the pollution in your surrounding environment. Your look may be laid back and chill, but you need durable clothing to take on your day. Better quality means less wear and tear.

STAPLES:

- Bikinis, bathing suits, and trunks

- Chopped up, crocheted and graphic Tees

- Skater shoes – like high tops, lace-ups, and slip-ons

Buy new: Vitamin A, Jeux De Vagues, Odina, Summersalt, KrelWear, Outerknown, Arbor, Faherty, Riz, United by Blue, HippyTree, Free Bella, Deep Blue Bag, FOKUS Green, Back Beat Rags, BeetxBeet, Human Revolution Clothing, Colorful Standard, Nomad Tribe, SZA'a Ctrl Fishing Company.

Buy used: Wasteland, GearTrade.com, Worn Wear (Patagonia),

Accessories: Allbirds lace-ups & Sugar Zeffers flip flops, MVMT, PACT, Krochet Kids, Keen, Colin Leslie, Mana Sidney Etnies, Jameson, Z Shoes Organic, Oka-B, Indosole, Shop Artesano, Sonder & Holliday Wander Wet Bags, Future Proof - Sunglasses (made from recycled refrigerators)

Yay! Outerknown Happy Tee, $48
Yay! SZA partnered with Champion to create Ctrl Fishing Company - sweatshirts bearing the Champion logo with colorful embroidery that reads "Sustainability Gang" and "Puck Flastic."

Celeb Crush: Pro surfer Kelly Slater built Outerknown, a sustainable surf-inspired men's line, from the ground up with very specific intentions to #MakeShiftHappen for a healthier fashion industry. As the face of many surf brands previous to Outerknown, Kelly's relationship to the destruction of the oceans is apparent in the choices he makes to implement better fabric choices in his own collection.

DEEP FRIED THOUGHTS

Sustainable Surf, #DeepBlueLife, Agalita, 5 Gyres, Parley for the Oceans, and the SurfRider Foundation are all organizations exposing fashion's damaging effect on our oceans. Microfibers, tiny little fiber particles that break off your clothes, are rinsed down the drain while washing your clothes. More specifically, plastic microfibers from items of clothing including bathing suits, and polyester T-shirts, as well as unregulated chemical dumping, are irreversibly f'n up the homes of ocean critters. Think about it this way: What your fish eats, you end up eating, too!

10. Sunday Brunch

Imagine you're hanging at a café or a fabulous restaurant, laughing, and talking about the weekend's festivities with friends, and enjoying the sunshine with a mimosa or chai latte in hand. Comfy, cozy, sassy, silly, mix and matchy. You can't go wrong when pulling out old favorites and pairing them with new finds. Catch up with friends, or even meet your partner's mom – think of it as "perfectly unpolished."

STAPLES:

- Comfortable sundresses
- Sun hats, sunglasses, and wicker purses
- Bright, floral, or pastel flowy pants
- Wedges, slides, and strappy sandals

Buy new: Bayou with Love, LA Relaxed, Krochet Kids, Peri (Pure Eco Rag Industry!), Kelly Lane, The Onikas, Sloane & Tate, Raven & Lily, Hazel & Rose, Whimsy + Row, Amour Vert, Arkins, Industry of All Nations, Loomstate, Orgotton, Amour Vert, Kaight, Eco Outfitters, Know Supply, SITA Couture

Buy used: Quirk, Black Rainbow, thredUP, Poshmark

Accessories: Sonder & Holliday, Zkano, White Rabbit (undies), Sokoloff (undies too)

WHAT TEE look FOR!
Yay! Alta Gracia Keila V-neck, $28

Celeb Crush: Actress Nikki Reed (FYI, crushing on hubby Ian Somerhalter too) launched Bayou with Love, a clothing line that uses chemical-free Cupro, a cellulose fiber made from recovered cotton waste among other fab options, and The Circular Collection (gold) with Love and Dell.

DEEP FRIED THOUGHTS

There is a disconnect between creators and makers for some brands. Do you know who made your clothes? If you haven't met the makers, you may want to look for brands with designers (and design teams) and boutique owners (and their team) who do have close relationships with their workers. Designers that work personally and directly with their clothing producers oftentimes have a uniquely contagious zest for life.

11. Yogi All Day

An average day may look a little something like this: hit the yoga studio in the wee hours of the morning, grab a smoothie after class, run errands into the afternoon, and then reward yourself by binging on reality TV in the evening – all while knowing your butt looks great the whole time. This is a multifaceted girl in a multifunctional outfit, for both her craziest and laziest days. Athleisure never looked and felt so good!

STAPLES:

- Convenient, comfortable, stretchy

- Form-fitting tanks, T-shirts, and pants

- Mix and match tops and bottoms

- Transitions easily from workouts to errands to drinks

Buy new: PACT, Boody, prAna, Teeki, Agathos Athleisure, RUMI X, Free Label, Girlfriend Collective, Threads for Thought

Buy used: Goodwill, Salvation Army

Accessories: Indosole (tire tread flip flops), Rossell & Co., Boody (undies for under yoga pants)

—— WHAT TEE LOOK FOR! ——

Yay! Commonwealth / Press Royal Apparel "Pittsburgh is Riveting" T-shirt, $25

Celeb Crush: Props to Vanessa Hudgens for sporting Teeki yoga pants around L.A.

DEEP FRIED THOUGHTS

EXTRA CRISPY BY TARYN HIPWELL

- Do I think that synthetic yoga pants are going to go away? NOPE.
- Do I think that fabric made from recycled plastic water bottles, PET (polyethylene terephthalate) is a good replacement for petroleum-based virgin fabric that off-gases toxic fumes? YEP.
- Do I think it would benefit all yogis to switch to loose-fitting natural fiber pants? YEP, (If only to stop making your body do extra work when it tries to ingest plastic into its pores).
- Do organic cotton and healthier natural fiber yoga pants exist? YEP! (Get on the PACT newsletter list for discounts and lots of sales)

Yay! Recycled PET works amazingly well when combined with heat press digital printing, a process that eliminates toxic dyes and water intensive printing processes. The designs adhere to the fibers when heated, which deter fading and pilling. Double win!

CHAPTER 4:

What's That Made of?

*Explaining the chemistry of **dyes and fibers** – and other nerdy fun facts*

So that brings us to our big question:

"What's in my tee?"

We hope this question serves as a jumping-off point for people to question what it is that they're putting on their bodies.

THIS IS WHAT'S IN YOUR TEE!

1. **It's All In The Ingredients:** *Exploring the chemistry of dyes and fibers*

2. **Top Toxic Additives:** *Introducing the BtL "F"ed Up Fashion 5*

3. **Not All Ingredients Are Created Equal**

4. **Non-Food Grade Dyes:** *Dyes that are to die for*

5. **Grocery List:** *What are the "Fab 5 Fabrics"?*

6. **Tasty Treats:** *Digging into "mouth-edible" and "body-edible" plant fabric*

7. **Leftovers:** *Recycling fabric and repurposing clothing*

8. **"What's in my tee?":** *Good vs. Evil*

9. **Beyond the Label's Top 10 Tenacious Tees**

IT'S ALL IN THE INGREDIENTS

Exploring the chemistry of dyes and fibers

By Karen Housel
Environmental scientist and founder of Sustainable Daisy fashion blog

A hazardous waste is a waste with properties that make it dangerous, or capable of having a harmful effect on human health or the environment.

I deal with pretty hardcore hazardous chemicals in my day job. I'm a hazmat specialist, which means I inspect environments with possible exposure to hazardous materials. I've seen my fair share of alarming things during inspections. I've seen toxic sludge at car battery recycling facilities and examined crushed leaded glass at e-waste refurbishers. But what gives me chills is the thought of damaging chemicals lurking in places I'm not expecting them to be, like my jackets, pajamas, or pillowcases. There's something sinister about fast fashion business owners who allow a level of exposure of hazardous chemicals to people who haven't the slightest idea of what they're being exposed to.

Brands trying to convince you that a certain level of toxicity in their clothing is tolerable, or doesn't even affect you, is bogus. Toxics in fashion should not be tolerated because there are plenty of non-toxic options available. According to a 2012 Greenpeace investigation, 20 of the world's most popular brands – Zara, H&M, and Levi's included – sell clothing containing hazardous chemicals, the production of which contributes to toxic water pollution. Since the revelation, H&M has committed to using only recycled or sustainably sourced materials in all their products by 2030. Levi's made a commitment to not emit any hazardous chemicals in their denim production processes by 2020, and Zara is working on a sustainable collection with eco-friendly fabrics. I find it amusing how quickly brands move to clean up their act after being called out. For me, it reinforces the power of accountability. No brand wants to be seen as unethical or irresponsible, perhaps purely for economic reasons, as brand damage can have a negative effect on sales. Still, I respect the transitions these companies are trying to make and I root for eco-curious companies.

TOP TOXIC ADDITIVES

Introducing: *The BtL "F"ed Up Fashion 5*

The Environmental Working Group (EWG) publishes their list of Dirty Dozen Endocrine Disruptors (fancy talk for hormone-disrupting chemicals) for the beauty industry, plus a separate rundown of the fruits and veggies you ought to buy organic. It's in that spirit that we decided to create **The BtL "F"ed Up Fashion 5**, a list of creepy chemicals to avoid when seeking healthy fashion.

In our next guidebook we will break down:

"Is it in my clothes?"

"How can I tell if it's in my clothes?"

"What chemicals should I look for?"

We are currently working with notable science experts, fabric experts, and organizations that push for safer fiber, dyes, and chemicals used in the fashion industry. As we learn, we will share more how-to solutions with you.

> *"As a woman with a history of autoimmune disease, I try to **reduce** my **exposure** to **immune-altering toxins,** especially those found in our clothes. I love shopping at **secondhand** stores because most of the chemicals have been washed out of them. Now that I'm pregnant and starting a family, I want to be mindful about my kids' clothes too. **Hand-me-downs** and **organic cotton** clothing from brands like Burt's Bees online will be my go-to choices!"*
>
> *– Robin Shirley, founder of the Take Back Your Health conference*

Yay! The simplest and most inexpensive way you can contribute to clean fashion is to choose a clean detergent (Ecos, Seventh Generation, The Honest Company) to wash your clothes. What goes down the drain matters.

BtL "F"ed Up Fashion 5
Top Toxic Additives

Azo Dyes	Chromium VI	Formaldehyde	NPEs and APEs	Phthalates
USE: pigment **ISSUE:** alters genetic material (DNA)	**USE:** catalyst **ISSUE:** carcinogen (capable of causing cancer)	**USE:** preservatives **ISSUE:** skin irritation / causes cancer	**USE:** detergent **ISSUE:** ocean pollution / fish infertility	**USE:** durability **ISSUE:** body disruptor / birth defects

Take a photo of The "F"ed Up Fashion 5 graphic, print it out, put it in your wallet and refer to it anytime you buy clothes. Think of it in the same way as you would a list of specific attributes you look for when buying a car (great gas mileage) or a new shampoo (sulfate-free). Here is a more in-depth breakdown so you can understand what to look for and what to avoid.

Azo Dyes

Azo dyes are uber pigmented, which look great for clothes, but have some not-so-great consequences. While many azo dyes are non-toxic, some are mutagens – chemicals that alter genetic material, like your DNA.

Chromium VI

Chromium VI also known as hexavalent chromium, is often used in leather tanning and as a catalyst (a substance that causes a chemical reaction to occur, but is not itself involved in the reaction) to disperse dyes, despite being a known carcinogen.

Formaldehyde

Formaldehyde is used to permanently press fabrics. It's also used in T-shirts to preserve the fabric, as well as fur, leather, and other animal hair fabrics, yet it causes skin, eye, nose, and throat irritation. High levels of exposure can cause throat spasms, fluid buildup in the lungs, burns, and even cancer. Yikes!

NPEs and APEs

NPEs and APEs are persistent chemicals that are great for surface tension and breaking down dirt, making them convenient for fast fashion retailers to wash and prepare clothing with. The shitty part is that byproducts of NPEs wash out into the ocean and mess with the hormones of fish, sometimes rendering them infertile.

Phthalates

Phthalates are added to clothes to increase a garment's flexibility, durability, and longevity. They're often found in common synthetic leather substitutes. Unfortunately, phthalates can cause birth defects and breast cancer, among other bodily disruptions (can you believe baby toys are made with this stuff?).

NOT ALL INGREDIENTS ARE CREATED EQUAL

THINK FABRIC FIRST:

Cotton, polyester, and wood-based fabrics are not produced, recycled, or processed in the same ways.

With the help of fashion industry experts, let's dive a little more deeply into the details of a few fabrics to equip you to make more informed decisions and feel proud of your next purchases.

Conventional Cotton vs. Organic Cotton vs. Recycled Cotton

At BtL events, we've noticed that people love to share how much cotton they wear. It's hard to have a conversation that deflates this excitement, even if we're trying to impart wisdom that's in their best interest. Simply put:

○ **Conventional** cotton is actually quite vile.

○ **Organic** cotton is healthy and clean for you and your body.

○ **Recycled** cotton is healthy and clean for the earth that you live on.

CONVENTIONAL COTTON

> *"Cotton is one of the* **most chemically toxic crops** *on the planet. Just because you don't eat it, it still is* **polluting** *our soil, water, and bodies. Panic if it's not organic."*
>
> *— Ryland Engelhart, mission fulfillment officer and co-owner of Cafe Gratitude, co-founder of educational nonprofit Kiss the Ground*

VS. ORGANIC COTTON

VS. RECYCLED COTTON

Recycled cotton can be created from both pre-consumer and post-consumer waste, like cutting room scraps and secondhand clothing, which is easily recycled into new fibers. Cutting room scraps from uniform factories can be sorted by color into separate bags. This is a bonus because when a company like Recover wants to recycle the fibers, they don't have to dye the fabric because the scraps are already color sorted. Post-consumer waste, like secondhand clothing, is not as easy to sort. This is because some fast fashion fabrics are either too weak to function well or are blends, so it's more difficult to create a consistent new fabric.

Synthetic fabric, whether it's virgin or recycled, is unhealthy not only for your body, but also the ocean, due to microfibers and unregulated dumping of toxic dyes. Finding a use for the plastics we fish out of the ocean and finding a way to reuse plastics before they even get to the ocean is important to reduce waste for a healthier world. We recommend always seeking out non-synthetic fabrics, but if you do opt for synthetic, look for recycled options to reduce your plastic contribution to landfill waste.

***"Synthetic fibers** overwhelmingly **dominate** apparel fiber consumption. They are entirely man-made and are derived from petroleum – that is, **crude oil**. Demand for polyester has steadily grown over the years. In 1980, only 5.2 million tons of polyester were produced globally, but by 2014, it had reached 46.1 million tons. Polyester production has **high environmental costs**, as does its disposal. Factories without wastewater treatment systems can release potentially **dangerous substances**, including antimony, cobalt, manganese salts, sodium bromide, and titanium dioxide.*

*So if you use synthetics, try switching to **recycled polyester,** the production of which consumes 70% less energy than virgin fiber. Almost all recycled polyester in textiles comes from **recycled plastic bottles**, not recycled clothes."*

– Information sourced from Common Objective: Do Better Fashion

Yay! Thread, a fabric brand, transforms discarded plastic bottles from the streets and canals of Haiti and Honduras into the most responsible fabrics on the planet. Every product made by Thread supports thousands of dignified jobs in developing countries and the U.S. Brands and designers use Thread's purpose-filled fabrics in their products, such as apparel, shoes, and accessories, to improve their social and environmental impact.

Yay! Arcadia Brown Cotton - Field to Fashion is a new initiative that unites farmers and stylist in order to preserve Acadiana roots and put it to use today.

Yay! Thread is also a certified B Corporation. B Corps meet the highest standards of verified social and environmental performance, public transparency, and legal accountability, and aspire to use the power of markets to solve social and environmental problems.

Viscose vs. Lenzing®

*"**Conventional viscose**, or **rayon**, is made from **cellulose** from **trees** and **plants**, which is processed with **heavy chemicals** like sodium hydroxide (caustic soda), carbon disulfide, and sulphuric acid. If not handled correctly, these chemicals can **cause harm** to those working with them. If not disposed of safely or reused through a closed loop process, but instead dumped into local rivers, they can have serious **negative environmental impacts**.*

*Instead, try switching to **TENCEL™** and **Lenzing™ Modal**, fabrics made via **solvent spinning** rather than conventional viscose methods. With these, there is an almost complete **recovery** of the solvent, the water used is also **recycled**, and its byproducts are key ingredients in the food and glass industries."*

— Information sourced from Common Objective: Do Better Fashion

Yay! TENCEL™ with Refibra™ technology, 100% post-industrial cotton scraps, recycled, turned to pulp; combined with TENCEL™ pulp, blended and turned into a new fiber. 80% of it is TENCEL™ and 20% is cotton. Refibra™ is the new TENCEL™ technology that addresses the need for a more circular economy in the textile industry.

Hemp

"I have a vision that everyone is in a Hemp tee by 2020."

— Robert Jungmann, president, CEO, and founder of Jungmaven

*"Hemp is an incredible **phytoremediation plant**, meaning that it helps restore balance and cleans soil, air, and water. In addition, hemp is one of the fastest growing plants on Earth and can **sequester excess atmospheric carbon** to help reverse climate change and clean the air we breathe. **Climate adaptation** is one of the greatest opportunities of our generation."*

— Jungmaven

In the past, all hemp was required to be grown outside of the U.S. Many countries including China grow hemp outside the U.S. Hemp and marijuana are both from the cannabis plant. The hope is that now that marijuana is legal in some states, the revitalization of hemp being grown for its fiber use will become a viable business in the future. Fingers crossed.

NON-FOOD GRADE DYES

Dyes to die for

What are some of the toxic things in the dye process that mess people up?

> **"Textile workers** may be exposed to **powder dyes** via inhalation during dye weighing or mixing operations, and the EPA is concerned about a number of **potential health hazards**, from exposure to dye dust.**"**
>
> – EPA, Textile Dye Weighing Monitoring Study, 1990

Greenpeace is campaigning to stop the fashion industry from poisoning our water sources with hazardous, persistent, and hormone-disrupting chemicals. Their "Detox My Fashion" initiative challenges top brands to make amends by working with their suppliers to eliminate all hazardous chemicals from the entirety of their supply chain. Future and current designers, please take note: it's easier to start "clean" and "healthy" from scratch, but if you're already established, it's not impossible to shift direction to "cleaner" pastures.

Yay! For those of you that want to dive deeper into the chemical side of dyes and fibers please check out the Greenpeace "Detox My Fashion" campaign. They have done extensive research far beyond the simplified basic "F"ed Up Fashion 5 list we've presented to you.

Ex. Greenpeace's 11 hazardous chemicals to eliminate:

- Alkylphenols
- Phthalates
- Azo dyes
- Chlorobenzenes
- Chlorinated solvents
- Chlorophenols
- Brominated and chlorinated flame retardants
- Organotin compounds
- Perfluorinated chemicals
- Short-chain chlorinated paraffins
- Heavy metals, like cadmium, lead, mercury, and chromium VI

"The **DETOX campaign** *has put a lot pressure on brands to* **ban all hazardous chemicals** *from their production. We think that DETOX is now* **the new industry baseline** *because in the six years since the launch of the campaign in 2011, forerunners of the textile sector went from total denial and opacity of their supply chain to* **transparency** *and the banning of all hazardous chemicals. The 80 commitments of global brands and retailers – most recently the UK supermarket giant, Tesco – show the rest of the industry that using hazardous chemicals is not an option anymore."*

– Kirsten Brodde, lead on Greenpeace's Detox My Fashion initiative

"Why is it that people that are conscious about one part of their lives **lack consciousness** *for the rest? Where's the* **disconnect**? *If I care about* **toxic colors** *in my food, why wouldn't I ask where the color in my clothing comes from? The language is very much the same in both industries when you consider subjects like* **waste (textile and food), Monsanto, labor rights issues, regional production** *and more. The Food & Fibers Project aims to ask people to consider that if they care about where their food comes from, just maybe they might consider where their clothing came from."*

– Amy Dufalut, Co-Founder of The Food & Fibers Project, Director of Communications at the Pratt Institute Brooklyn Fashion + Design Accelerator.

We asked our dye experts their opinions and here's what they said:

What dye companies and fabric treatment companies offer kickass sustainable options?

Jeff Wilson, senior business development manager in sustainability, NSF, and formerly Textile Exchange, weighs in:

- **Archroma:** *A dye company that offers a host of sustainable dyes, including a line called "Natural Colors"*
- **ColorZen:** *A pre-treatment company that works at the cotton fiber stage to enable the dyeing of cotton fabric by utilizing fewer inputs – especially water and energy*
- **Dyecoo:** *A dye technology company with super compressed CO_2 and waterless dye technology for synthetic fabrics*
- **Huntsman Chemical:** *A chemical company with multiple products like Archroma; collaborated with Dyecoo on dyes for synthetics by using the super compressed CO_2 technology*
- **Novozymes:** *A company that uses enzyme-based pre-treatments to reduce dye input*

*"Almost four years ago, I was in a place of learning, seeing and truly understanding the apparel industry's **impact on the environment**. At the same time, I knew that my son was going to have to **face the mess** that we as an industry had been creating. This couldn't be what we left behind for him and **future generations**. I spoke at length about this to our Director of Production and told her we wouldn't go on like this. The rest is history."*

– Mara Hoffman, fashion designer

Do you think small brands can incorporate natural dyes to their dye processes more easily? Are natural dyes scalable for large brands? And why are natural dyes important?

Kathy Hattori, *the President of Botanical Colors LLC, weighs in:*

*"Based on the **global consumption** of textiles worldwide and the color needed for them, the demand for natural dyes, as well as low-impact dyes, is growing. The way that conventional color is applied to clothes is broken. **'Wet processing,'** as **industrial dyeing** is called, is one of the top polluters in the world, consuming enormous amounts of energy, water, and petrochemical-based colorants.*

***Botanical Colors** supplies artisans and in the fashion industry with the materials and know-how to dye textiles in a way that **uses less water, is non-toxic and biodegradable**, and draws its incomparable color palette from humble plants and natural sources. All colors are sustainably derived, many from agricultural and food waste products.*

*Along with our beautiful natural dyes, we fully support the reshoring movement to **bring textile jobs back** to the U.S. The wonderful thing about working with U.S. manufacturing is American know-how, scalability starting from the sample runs through large volume production, quick turnarounds, and American jobs."*

- Kathy Hattori, President of Botanical Colors LLC

GROCERY LIST

How to shop for clothes like you're shopping for food. Ingredients! Ingredients! Ingredients!

> *"Learning the source of the fibers in one's clothing is important, and it's not just because of the **negative environmental impact** caused by the growing of **conventional cotton** with **herbicides** and **pesticides**, which then enter our soil and water systems. The **chemicals poison** workers and people living in communities by the farms. There are also residual chemicals that remain on the garment, only to then be **absorbed into the skin** during wear, which can **cause health problems.**"*
>
> – Matt Boelk, co-founder of Groceries Apparel

CERTIFIED ORGANIC COTTON
Pesticide-free, herbicide-free, and GMO-free farming lessens the toxic grip that companies like Monsanto and Cargill have on our global society. Conventionally grown cotton is one of the most polluting crops in the world and leads to toxic dumping into our water supplies, oceans, and soils. Organic cotton farms support fair trade, healthier working conditions, and a safer end product for the consumer.

RECYCLED COTTON
Cotton recycling prevents unnecessary waste and is a more responsible option than outright disposal. Our 100% Post-industrial Recycled Cotton Jersey comes from discarded yarn and fabric, mostly the salvage from weaving and fabric from factory cutting rooms.

EUCALYPTUS
This fiber is made from responsibly-sourced eucalyptus trees from South Africa and California grown on low-grade land that's unusable for food production. The man-made fabric is created through the use of nanotechnology in a closed-loop process that recovers or decomposes all of its solvents and emissions.

HEMP
This versatile fiber is fast-growing, requires very little water, is naturally pest-resistant, and produces more fiber yield per acre than any other source. It's antibacterial, biodegradable, and resistant to mold, saltwater, and ultraviolet light.

RECYCLED PLASTIC
Recycling plastic decreases our dependence on oil as a raw material source. This fiber is important because the act of harvesting it actually cleans the environment. Recycling also curbs the amount of trash being dumped, prolonging landfill life. Reducing toxic emissions from the constant flow of landfill incinerators lessens the advance of global warming.

Take a photo of The "Fab 5 Fabrics" print it out, put it in your wallet, and refer to it anytime you buy clothes.

1. *Top and pants are recycled plastic*
2. *Bra is organic cotton and spandex*
3. *Sweatshirt is recycled plastic and the white shirt is organic cotton*
4. *Eucalyptus beanie and recycled cotton / recycled dress*

P.52 PHOTO DETAILS

TASTY TREATS

Digging into "body-edible" and "mouth-edible" plant fabric

Body-edible plant based fibers – Plants that are used to make fabric: cotton, flax, jute, wood pulp, hemp, and bamboo

Mouth and body-edible food and food waste fibers – Fibers originally intended for food consumption. The fibers may derive from plant waste including skins, leafs, stalks, and things like orange peels considered to be waste from orange juice

`BANANA` banana peel fabric - Abaca/Banana Fibers

`COFFEE` recycled coffee grounds fabric - S.Café (Victoria's Secret)

`COCONUT` coconut leaf fabric - Cocona (Adidas)

`CORN` renewable corn-derived glucose fabric - Dupont

Yay! Linda Loudermilk, one of the great eco fashion innovators, tested out some of the first corn fabric on the market 10+ years ago. She recalled, "The first time I washed the corn fabric, it came out looking like potato chips..." Years later, there have been great breakthroughs. Thank you LL for pushing fabric manufacturers to do better!

`MUSHROOM` mushroom leather - Mycoworks

`NETTLE` nettle as a healing fiber - Seam Sirens

`ORANGE` citrus juice byproduct fabric - Orange (Ferragamo) Fiber

Yay! Global Change Award WINNER Orange Fiber

`PINEAPPLE` pineapple leaf leather fabric - Piñatex (Worn by Liv Firth to the 2017 MET Gala)

`SEAWEED` seaweed, a cellulosic fabric - SeaCell

`SUGAR` derived from renewable sugarcane, SweetFoam™

`YEAST` harnessing proteins found in nature to create fibers and fabrics with both practical and revolutionary uses, starting with spider silk. "Proteins" are produced in large quantities through fermentation, using yeast, sugar, and water - Bolt Threads (Stella McCartney)

Yay! Biotech Gets The Luxury Nod With Bolt Threads X Stella McCartney Tie-Up, announced by Forbes

Yay! Leonardo Dicaprio invests in Allbirds and shouts out the Sugar Zeffers flip-flops.

KOMBUCHA DIY vegan leather. Make it yourself with a kombucha tea scoby.

WINE DIY bio-leather made of fermented wine - Vegeatextiles

Yay! Wine bio fabric · (WATCH: TED - Suzanne Lee: Grow your own clothes)

In future guidebooks, Beyond the Label will break down the growing process of each of the produce and crops listed above to open up the discussion over pesticide use and other questionable chemicals. Eventually we'd like to instigate clean, healthy, and non-GMO fiber standards in all aspects of the natural fiber processes. And we will introduce you to Agraloop, a circular and regenerative bio-refinery that converts food crop waste into valuable fiber and industrial products. Yeah, we're going to get downright nerdy in the next guidebook.

> *"**The Agraloop** is regenerative systems design. It is a **closed-loop bio-refinery** that produces its own power and bio-chemistry intrinsically from the food crop waste inputs. The system **returns surplus bio-energy to local communities**, as well as providing **organic fertilizer** and **bio-pesticide** back to farms to support the fertility cycle. Current food crop derived fiber products are produced in linear systems that use caustic chemical agents for processing."*
>
> *– Agraloop*

Yay! The Circular Systems team, Ytizac Goldstein CTO and Geoff Kind COO were runners up for the Global Change Award for Agraloop. They were selected for the first batch of the Fashion for Good accelerator program, and the first innovation ever to present at the Fashion for Good center during their unveiling.

Super Yay! Agraloop is a WINNER of the Global Change Award 2018.
"WE TRANSFORM FOOD-CROP WASTE INTO VALUABLE NATURAL FIBER PRODUCTS."
Including, but not limited to apple fabric.

LEFTOVERS

Recycling fabric and repurposing clothing

> **"Resource efficiency** is key if we are to survive, much less thrive, as a species. Our current take/make/waste linear extractive systems are literally **killing us**, and we will **not have sufficient resources** in coming decades to continue at anywhere near the current **pace of consumption** and market growth relative to **growing populations."**
>
> – Isaac Nichelson, founder of Sustainable Source Studios

RECYCLED FIBER FABRIC is made by physically grinding up fabric or other materials to create a new, virgin fabric.

This is a list of **FABRIC BRANDS** that recycle waste to make a virgin fabric which reduces landfill mass.

- **Recover** Upcycled Textile System turns textile waste into valuable new yarns for many life-cycles. **Yay! H&M**

- **Fabscrap** is a non-profit, 501(c)3 organization rethinking commercial textile waste by providing convenient pickup of unwanted textiles from N.Y.C. businesses. We ensure maximum diversion from landfill by utilizing the most current recycling technologies and engaging the local creative community in reuse." **Yay! Levi's**

- **Evernu** makes fabric from post-consumer clothing waste (secondhand clothing) **Yay! Timberland**

- Pittsburgh-based **Thread International** turns trash from the poorest neighborhoods in the world into purpose-filled, recycled fabric.

- **Bionic Yarn:** Parley for the Ocean and Pharrell have partnered to amplify the use of the recycled ocean plastic fabric (yes, plastic pulled out of the ocean!). **Yay! G-Star RAW**

- Textile company **Eclat's** main goal is to help U.S.A. Market start ups, mid-size and growing companies to a stable growth. How? By offering lower minimums, (Ex. 1 roll or 500 yard minimums vs. 10,000 yard minimums). **Yay! Teeki is sold at Urban Outfitters.**

- **Repreve** helps turn recycled plastic bottles into amazing products we can use and wear every day, but it starts with you each time you recycle. **Yay! Volcom NEW FUTURE - The ongoing efforts of turning sustainability commitments into actions.**

- **Ecoalf** clothing is made of recycled materials like plastic bottles and fishing net because, as they say, "There is no planet B."

RECYCLING FABRIC is a process in which pre-existing usable excess fabric is cut up to make clothing and accessories.

This is a list of ***FASHION BRANDS*** that recycle fabric waste to make unique items, which reduces landfill mass.

- **FahMina** uses recycled leather from the shoe industry to make rock star accessories.

- **Reformation** uses recycled deadstock fabric in their boho chic maxi dresses.

- **Ten Thousand Villages**, which is also fair trade, uses recycled woven sari fabric to make hats.

REPURPOSED clothes are made by deconstructing and reconstructing existing clothes.

This is a list of **FASHION BRANDS** that recycle secondhand clothing to reduce landfill mass.

- **Hipsters for Sisters:** Jeans get a second life as recycled denim "hands and shoulder free" waist purses (fancy fanny pack-esque).

- **H&M's Close the Loop initiative:** Secondhand clothing is made into new garments.

- **Loopwork:** Portland Trail Blazers jerseys are reimagined into backpacks, scarves, and jackets.

- **Preloved:** Great options featuring reclaimed vintage, deadstock, and overrun fabrics.

- **Urban Outfitters' Urban Renewal line:** Vintage clothes are chopped up into fresh designs.

---

*"**Sustainability** allows for those with **maximum creativity** but **minimum capital** to be a part of the fashion world. Tools for a beginner's sustainable success: **dumpsters for diving, charity thrift shops for collecting, scissors for shearing, sewing needles to stitch.**"*

— Lorrie Ivas, associate professor of business, retail, and fashion at Santa Monica College

---

BtL gear can be found at LABeyondtheLabel.com. These items were made in partnership with UCLA, Santa Monica College, MetaWear, LA Relaxed, SITA Couture at FIDM - LA Textile Show / FGI event. BtL's Original Concert Couture Concept Sample tent jackets were made from repurposed tents left behind at a music festival.

UPCYCLING occurs when material items considered to be waste are torn up and reconstructed into clothing and accessories.

This is a list of **WEIRD STUFF** created into unique items by recycling waste from other unrelated industries, which reduces landfill mass.

- Totes and bags crafted from **discarded Alaska and Southwest Airline seats** by Looptworks

- The Deep Blue Bag is a sustainably-sourced up-cycled urban adventure bag made of **wetsuits, sails, climbing ropes collected from Yosemite**

- Jewelry made from **board games and old computer parts** are everywhere on Etsy.

- Chemical-free, dyed **fish leather** wallets at Sea Accessories

- Belts, bags, and rocker accessories made from **inner tube tires** at Chic Made Consciously (CMC)

- Metal bracelets designed from **luxury car metal** at Crash Jewelry

- Crocheted, reusable bags made from **plastic bags** at Chikumbuso Women and Orphan Project

- Belts and totes made of **fire hoses** at Uncommon Goods

- Pins made of **computer parts** in the shape of Mary Poppins at TechWears

Yay! Jessica frequents Clothes Swap in L.A. clothing exchanges and she has a blog called *Adventures in Waste.*

The first EVER **Beyond the Label Fashion Show Team** excited to have blown minds. Taryn is wearing a dress by **Reformation** made of velvet burnout deadstock fabric. Textile recycling at its sassiest!

RECYCLING CLOTHING:

*This is a list of **WAYS YOU CAN RECYCLE CLOTHING** to reduce landfill mass.*

- **Clothing Swaps:** Shop from the excess of your friends' closets for free!

- **Clothing Rentals**: Consider renting. Clothing rentals are not just for tuxedos. It's a great option for one-time-wear occasions: Proms, weddings, speaking.

- **DIY:** Patch, mend, chop, and thrash your clothes into something new.

- **I:CO Bins:** If your clothes are really ready to move into their next phase of life, you can drop them off in I:CO-branded clothing recycle bins at several major retail stores. Wearable items are resold, some items are made into rags, and what can't be resold or reused is ground up for carpet padding and insulation.

- **Resale Shops:** Frequent vintage boutiques, secondhand stores, charitable organizations thrift shops, and consignment shops.

"What's in My Tee?"

Shoppers often ask the BtL Team: **"What am I actually paying for?"** *Below is a checklist of criteria to consider when shopping for a healthier style of life. Remember that what you're investing in is the removal of toxic chemicals for a healthier supply chain, higher standards of production, ethical certifications, and where it was produced.*

- ○ People (supply chain)
- ○ Planet (location)
- ○ Profit (brand transparency)
- ○ Fabric
- ○ Dye
- ○ Printing
- ○ What else you can do!

Yay! Passionate CSU student, Kristin Breakell, exhibited an incredible series of posters in the LSC Arts Auxillary where the Beyond the Label T-shirt Exchange and Upcycling Lab was held.

What's in a typical $5 T-shirt?

- **Fabric:** Arsenic, bleach, formaldehyde, pesticides, petroleum, and cancer-causing agents

- **Dye:** Airborne, ingestible toxic mordants, cadmium, lead, mercury, and chromium VI

- **Printing:** Plastic

- **People:** Workers in slave-like conditions who are forced to have direct contact with the aforementioned hazardous dye and fabric chemicals

- **Planet:** Unregulated chemical dumping and pesticide run-off which f's up water sources

- **Profit:** Upper management live like kings, while employees sleep on concrete floors as seen in the mini-series, "Sweatshop"

- **Wearability:** stretches out, pills, fades after 5 washes and loses its value quickly. Its the one you pick out for date night and have to toss it back because the seam snapped on the side as you try to pull it over your head

What's in a Yay! tee?

Let's dissect one of our favorites, the women's v-neck from PACT for $15.99.

- **Fabric:** GOTS (Global Organic Textile Standard) certified organic cotton

- **Dye:** GOTS certified non-toxic dyes and/or vegetable dyes

- **Printing:** None

- **People:** Fair Trade certified! Safe, healthy conditions for fabric, dye, and production workers based in India

- **Planet:** Water filtration systems keep harmful toxins from polluting nearby clean water sources

- **Profit:** Employees are paid a wage that covers expenses and investments in their education and their children

- **Wearability:** Holds structure, drapes well, lasts 20, 30, sometimes 50+ washes and 20, 30, sometimes 50+ wears. Super selfie worthy and feels so good against your skin – you'll want to fall asleep in it and never take it off

TOP 10 TENACIOUS TEES

This list includes one **TENACIOUS TEE BRAND** per **PERSONAL STYLE** listed in the **"What Shall I Wear Today?"** section. Each brand has made shift happen with a T-shirt, and we appreciate all of them for their commitment, compassion, and transparency! The value of a tee is unique based on:

- Quality of the sustainable fabric, dyeing, and ethical sewing
- Location the tee was designed
- Location (city, state, or country) the fabric was produced
- Location (city, state, or country) the garment was sewn and assembled
- Location (city, state, or country) from which the finished garment was distributed
- Regulations enforced in each city, state, or country
- Wages paid by each individual brand as well as fair wage minimums vs. minimum wage (many countries' minimum wage is unlivable).
- Certifications for the fabric, dyeing and/or garment production
- Markup (retail in a store vs. direct to consumer): directly selling to the shopper at the wholesale markup is typically half of retail price. When a brand sells directly, you as an informed consumer will get a better price for better quality.

BOHO CHIC - PACT
Yay! PACT Women's V-Neck, $15.99
Fabric: 100% GOTS-certified organic cotton
Origin: India
Reasoning: Organic is better for the planet, farmers, and factory workers!

BOOTCAMP - PATAGONIA
Yay! Patagonia Women's Blythewood Tee, $35
Fabric: Tri-blend jersey (50% polyester, 25% organic cotton, 25% TENCEL™)
Origin: Pratibha Syntex Ltd. Textile Mill & Sewing Factory in India
Reasoning: For being transparent about fibers, fabric, and production way before it was cool

CLUBGOER - SCIENCE OF APPAREL
Yay! Science of Apparel Non-Binary Galileo Tee, $48
Fabric: Compact Pima
Origin: New York HQ
Reasoning: For having the word "science" in their name, for incorporating scientific studies in their branding, and for using the term "non-binary" to embrace all genders

THE F'N BOSS - GROCERIES APPAREL

Yay! Groceries Apparel Men's Contrast Poc Crew T-shirt, $44
Fabric: 50% organic cotton and 50% recycled plastic bottles
Origin: Made in L.A.!
Reasoning: For introducing the concept of fiber content of a T-shirt as "Ingredients" over 6 years ago, for shifting T-shirt production in L.A. forever, and for passionately sourcing fiber ingredients and fabrics that feed the body and soul!

HIPSTER - JUNGMAVEN

Yay! Jungmaven Stone Washed & Distressed Baja SS 7 oz - Unisex, $55
Fabric: 55% hemp and 45% organic cotton
Origin: Made in the U.S.A.
Reasoning: "We broke it in for you!" Working their fabric to appear distressed in a high-fashion hipster way, attention to detail, and their desire to get hemp tees on everyone!

JEANS & T-SHIRT - BTL'S METAWEAR & LA RELAXED

Yaaaaaaay! Beyond the Label / MetaWear Nutrition Label Tee, $28
Fabric: organic cotton and seaweed dyes
Origin: Made in the U.S.A.
Reasoning: See image below with certifications

Yaaaaaaay! Beyond the Label / LA Relaxed Nutrition Label Tee, $28
Fabric: Recover
Origin: Made in L.A.
Reasoning: See image below with certifications

Yaaaaaaay! Beyond the Label / LA Relaxed Comical Care Label "Trashed Up" Tee, $44
Fabric: TENCEL™
Origin: Made in L.A.
Reasoning: "Touch me I'm Soft!" is an understatement. The creative cut of LA Relaxed garments are innovative and fun.

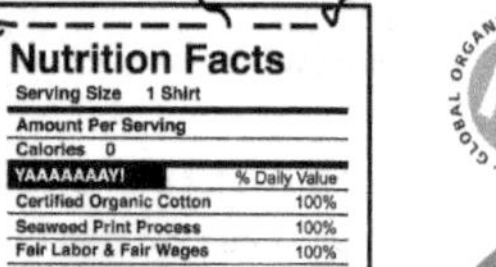

PROM & RED CARPET - EILEEN FISHER

Yay! Eileen Fisher Micro TENCEL™, micro rib stitch, round neck slim top T-shirt, $112
Fabric: TENCEL™
Origin: Spun outside in Atlanta, knitted in Montreal, cut and sewn in New York City
Reasoning: Eileen Fisher is on the front lines of sustainable fashion education as well as leading the way to making natural dyes scalable.

ROCKER CHIC - ROYAL APPAREL & COMMONWEALTH PRESS

Yay! Commonwealth Press & Royal Apparel "Pittsburgh is Riveting" T-shirt, $25
Fabric: 50% organic, 50% recycled poly
Origin: Printed in Pittsburgh
Reasoning: Commitment to educating willing customers to understanding sustainable solutions and always looking for new technologies to improve printing processes

SKATER/SURFER - OUTERKNOWN

Yay! Outerknown Happy Tee, $48
Fabric: 100% organic Peruvian pima cotton
Origin: Global, HQ in L.A. (manufacturer, Cotton Bergman Rivera is known for their farm to floor production process).
Reasoning: Kelly Slater uses his global recognition to educate the surf community about how the fabric in their clothes can have a positive effect on the oceans.

YOGI ALL DAY - PRANA

Yay! prAna Lynette Top, $59
Fabric: 50% organic cotton and 50% recycled polyester
Origin: Global
Reasoning: Commitment to offering non-petroleum synthetic options for Yogis and Bootcamp peeps.

NEWEST T-SHIRT FINDS:
Yay! Industry of All Nations - this store is like a science museum. Check out what indigo looks like before its made into a dye. All their fabrics are kind to nature. Watch their video to learn about the Clean Clothes Project.
Yay! Known Supply, launched by Krochet Kids. Stop guessing about who made your tees.
Yay! Check out LABeyondtheLabel.com for shopper shared up to date new finds, clothing, and the impact of your purchases.

CHAPTER 5:

Who Gives a Shift?
*Introduction to **organizations making shift happen***

We're tired of hearing that:

"NO ONE GIVES A SHI(F)T ABOUT SUSTAINABLE FASHION."

WE GIVE A "F"!!

Things you have the power to affect with your shopping habits:

Become a sustainable superhero! You have the power to save people, animals, and the planet simply by shifting your shopping.

- Air pollution
- Animal cruelty
- Cancer, leukemia, and brain tumors
- Modern day slavery (yes, this is still happening)
- Oil, gas, and petroleum usage (transportation and synthetic fabrics)
- Plastic pollution in the oceans
- Waste in landfills
- Water pollution vs. clean, drinkable water
- Water scarcity vs. excessive water usage
- Women's rights

Shoppers that give a shit, make brands give a shift.

There's a lot of conflicting information out there. Organizations are keen to say and look like they "do good," but oftentimes brands stretch the truth or even create bogus certifications to "greenwash" themselves for good publicity. Our goal is to guide you to trusted organizations, apps, and innovators working in various sectors of the sustainable fashion industry.

*"The most important part of **activism** is to act. Make small and big **changes** to your life to live in line with **your values.** That way you are a part of the change and **lead by example."***

– Lauren Fay, Founder and CEO at The New Fashion Initiative

Sustainable Fashion Organizations That #MakeShiftHappen

BEYOND THE LABEL

(L.A., GLOBAL)

Beyond the Label (BtL) started as a partnership with TEDxLA to educate Angelenos about the true health, social, and environmental costs of their fashion purchases. BtL is now a charitable organization, that which through **events and GUIDEBOOKS**, encourages shoppers to consider **"What's in my tee?"** to think about what their T-shirt is made of, and how it affects the world, the workers, and ourselves. Think fabric first!

> *" For too long, sustainability has been but an add-on conversation in fashion education, a nod to the conversation currently happening in the industry. However, **sustainability** should now be at the **core** of any fashion business or design course. It's implications are far reaching across the **fashion supply chain**, including **product development, manufacturing** and **omni-channel retail**. Students should understand that sustainability isn't just about the environment and **fair trade**, it's necessary to achieve long-term financial success."*
>
> *– Joshua Williams, Professor and Fashion Business Expert*

BROOKLYN FASHION + DESIGN ACCELERATOR

(BROOKLYN, NY)

BFDA is an **ethical fashion and design hub** that provides designers with **resources** to develop their ideas into successful businesses.

CALIFORNIA FASHION ASSOCIATION (CALIFORNIA)

The **CFA forum** addresses issues of concern to the industry as a whole for the benefit of manufacturers, suppliers, educational institutions, allied associations, and all apparel-related businesses.

The COLLABORATORY (S.F.)

Collborative + Laboratory = Collaboratory. There's a new generation of apparel makers committed to the important issues. What if they could learn from industry insiders and veterans? What if they could work with a community of peers and experts to tackle social and environmental challenges? NOW THEY CAN. (Levi Strauss & Co.)

COMMON OBJECTIVE (LONDON)

CO is an intelligent **business network** for the fashion industry. Their technology matches members with the connections and resources they need to succeed – and makes it easier for them to work in the most sustainable way.

◒ **Yay! For those of you who have followed Ethical Fashion Forum or the SOURCE guide, Common Objective is the next phase of their journey.**

CONSCIOUS CHATTER (GLOBAL)

A conversational, informative **podcast** from host **Kestrel Jenkins** that digs into the layers of stories, meaning, and potential impact connected to the clothes we wear.

> **"Audio** has a powerful way of allowing people to **join an unfamiliar conversation** without feeling overwhelmed by its complexities. I believe the podcasting medium has the unique power to give people **free access to information** about topics they may not otherwise learn about. When it comes to making an impact on the **future of fashion**, audio gives people like me the opportunity to connect with larger audiences, and to **expand beyond** the often niche **sustainable fashion bubble**. The up-and-coming generations want to know the stories behind their stuff. They are **asking questions** about where things come from, how they are made and who is connected to the process. They are asking for **transparency**. This is inspiring, and it motivates me to continue learning and sharing information on the players who are pushing to change what the future of fashion looks like.**"**
>
> – Kestrel Jenkins, host and producer of Conscious Chatter podcast

COUNCIL FOR TEXTILE RECYCLING (U.S.)

CTR is **nonprofit organization** dedicated to raising public awareness about the importance of textile recycling and reducing the amount of used clothing and other post-consumer textile waste being sent to landfills.

ECO FASHION WEEK (VANCOUVER & SEATTLE)

EFW is a **not-for-profit organization** that aims to present the solutions and innovations for a more responsible fashion industry.

    ○ **Yay! After many years of putting on fashion shows in Vancouver, Eco Fashion Week has begun doing shows in Seattle as well.**

ECO FASHION WEEK AUSTRALIA (AUSTRALIA)

Perth-based Australian eco fashion designer/visual artist Zuhal Kuvan-Mills of Green Embassy has taken her passion for slow fashion to a new level with the creation of international **Eco Fashion Week** Australia.

ECOLOGIQUE (S.F.)

APR and **marketing business** dedicated to expanding the reach of sustainable fashion.

ECOSESSIONS® (GLOBAL)

A series of global sustainability, green, **eco events.**

> **"Fast fashion** is giving new meaning to the phrase **'fashion victims.'** In the traditional sense, we are talking about people who slavishly follow fashion trends, but quite literally we should be addressing the millions of **garment workers** who are subjected to **dangerous health, safety, and working conditions."**
>
> – Erin Brown, L.A. Ambassador for EcoSessions

ELLEN MACAUTHUR FOUNDATION (U.K., GLOBAL)

The Ellen MacArthur Foundation is a British registered charity with the stated aim of inspiring a generation to re-think, re-design & build a positive future through the framework of a circular economy.

    ○ **Yay! Stella McCartney supports circular textiles economy with Ellen MacArthur Foundation. And yes, this does include Adidas by Stella McCartney. It's time to radically rethink fashion. Circular is the new Black.**

ETHICAL CLOTHING AUSTRALIA (AUSTRALIA)

An **accreditation body** that works collaboratively with local textile, clothing, and footwear companies to ensure their Australian supply chains are transparent and legally compliant.

ETHICAL FASHION SHOW BERLIN (BERLIN)

The Kraftwerk Berlin becomes the hotspot for urban zeitgeist, eco-fair lifestyle and fashion. In the new location, the **Ethical Fashion Show Berlin** presents progressive streetwear, and casual wear labels during Berlin Fashion Week. With a clear focus on design and sustainability, the show brings together top players from the eco fashion segment.

FABSCRAP (N.Y.C.)

FABSCRAP is a **non-profit**, 501(c)3 organization rethinking commercial textile waste by providing convenient **pickup of unwanted textiles** from N.Y.C. businesses. "We ensure maximum diversion from landfill by utilizing the most current recycling technologies and engaging the local creative community in reuse."

FACTORY45 (U.S. & CANADA)

An online **accelerator program** that helps propel sustainable apparel companies from idea to launch. Factory45 has helped entrepreneurs from all over the U.S. and Canada learn how to successfully bring an apparel company to market.

FAIR TRADE FASHION SHOW (L.A.)

FTFS brings together industry leaders, artisan fashion, and the local **L.A. community to provide impactful solutions to global issues.** This unique project uses fashion as a platform for inspiration and action, celebrating the power of everyday purchases to support sustainability.

FAIR TRADE LA (L.A.)

FTLA is a **membership-based nonprofit organization** that includes individuals, business members, university and student groups, faith-based members, and nonprofit organizations.

OBJECTIVES:

- Create fair trade towns, colleges, universities, congregations, and schools in cities throughout Los Angeles County and surrounding areas
- Inform L.A. shoppers about fair trade as an aspect of social justice and develop conscious shoppers
- Bring more fair trade products to the L.A. area
- Connect members of the L.A. community with others who have similar environmental, social, and economic concerns.

FASHION 4 DEVELOPMENT (D.C.)

F4D is a **global platform** promoting positive social change by harnessing the power of the fashion and beauty industries to implement creative strategies for sustainable economic growth and independence of communities worldwide, all through the expression of fashion.

FASHION HEROES (GLOBAL)

For this **video series**, brought to you by the filmmakers behind the documentary *RiverBlue*, **sustainable fashion experts** speak about their passion for their work and how it can help move the fashion industry forward. The FashionHeroes.eco website is a destination for people to discuss sustainable fashion, learn which brands are making strides, and see how we can all make wiser shopping choices.

FASHION INCUBATOR SAN FRANCISCO (S.F.)

FiSF is a Bay Area **incubator program** created to accelerate emerging apparel and accessories design businesses, while supporting economic growth and job creation.

FASHION REVOLUTION (LONDON, U.S., & GLOBAL)

A **global movement** that runs all year long. Fashion Revolution celebrates fashion as a positive influence while also scrutinizing industry practices and raising awareness of the fashion industry's most pressing issues. They aim to show that change is possible and encourage those who are on a journey to create a more ethical and sustainable future for fashion.

FASHION REVOLUTION USA (U.S.)

We believe in a fashion industry that values people, the environment, creativity and profit in equal measure. We want to **unite people and organizations to work together** towards radically changing the way our clothes are sourced, produced and consumed, so that our clothing is made in a safe, clean and fair way. We believe that collaborating across the whole value chain – from farmer to consumer – is the only way to transform the industry. Our mission is to bring everyone together to make that happen.

○ **Yay! Fashion Revolution Week's #whomademyclothes campaign is in April, which falls on the anniversary of the Rana Plaza factory collapse - an incident that killed 1,134 garment workers and injured many more on April 24th, 2013. That is the day Fashion Revolution was born. During this week, brands and producers are encouraged to respond with the hashtag #imadeyourclothes and to demonstrate transparency in their supply chain.**

FASHION TAKES ACTION (CANADA)

Fashion Takes Action is Canada's only **nonprofit** that focuses on sustainability, which advances sustainability in the entire fashion system through education, awareness and collaboration.

FASHION SHAKEDOWN (N.Y.C)

Fashion Shakedown was created to highlight and **recognize the various fashion companies** who are changing the way the fashion industry has been operating for decades. Fashion Shakedown was created with you, the student, the researcher, the entrepreneur, the established business owner in mind. By showcasing the new industry best practices, you can more quickly work to shift priorities and see the possibilities for your own businesses and choices.

FIBERSHED (S.F.)

Fibershed develops **regional and regenerative fiber system**. They envision the emergence of an international system of regional textile communities that enliven connection and ownership of 'soil-to-soil' textile processes. Both fiber and food systems now face a drastically changing climate, and must utilize the best of time-honored knowledge and available science for their long-term ability to thrive.

FOOD & FIBERS PROJECT (U.S.)

Given that the conversation about slow fashion has yet to gain the momentum of slow food, in order to be advocates for slow fashion, we want to **help consumers make the connections between what they eat and what they wear.** Because of this, The Food and Fibers Project aims to use written and visual media to:

- Make the connection between what we eat and what we wear

- Preserve cultural heritage showcasing what we risk losing in the face of fast food and fast fashion.

- Look at the resources that we often call waste in both food and fiber, showing how this is in fact a new harvest

- Reconnect with the land through what we eat and what we wear

- Reconnect with the people responsible for what we eat and what we wear

- Promote sustainable agricultural and harvest practices in both food and fiber

FREE THE SLAVES (D.C.)

Since its founding in 2000, the mission of Free the Slaves (FTS) has been to **liberate slaves** and change the conditions that allow slavery to persist. FTS helps communities chart their own path toward **sustainable freedom** based on their unique needs and circumstances. The organization strengthens the capacity of grassroots organizations, government agencies, advocacy coalitions, and the media to take action. FTS also supports vulnerable communities through rights education, mobilization, and increasing access to education, vocational training, and essential services. FTS currently operates in six countries: Haiti, Senegal, Ghana, Democratic Republic of the Congo, India and Nepal.

○ **Free the Slaves' annual Fashion for Freedom Campaign brings together the worlds of fashion and human rights, aiming to create a space where fashion lovers and activists can celebrate the efforts of ethical brands and bring awareness to atrocities such as slavery in the fashion industry.**

GALERIE.LA (L.A.)

Galerie.LA is a fully immersive ethical concept shop where customers are invited to shop their values with ease. Thoughtfully curated styles feature emerging brands who focus on eco-friendly, artisan, vegan and local production.

GLOBAL FASHION AGENDA / COPENHAGEN FASHION SUMMIT (COPENHAGEN)

First and foremost, the Global Fashion Agenda is a fashion platform that relays expert knowledge to mainstream fashion executives and creatives, taking sustainability out of the lab and into the boardroom, thereby influencing decision making at a strategic and operational level. Meanwhile, industry leaders gather at the **Copenhagen Fashion Summit** to discuss how they can contribute to the world overall.

GOOD ON YOU (AUSTRALIA)

An **app providing ethical brand ratings** for more than 1,100 fashion brands, based on how they treat workers, the planet, and animals.

> *"Great **style** and beautiful products **shouldn't cost people their lives** or the **health** of our **environment**. We want to change the way people buy fashion so that businesses have strong incentives to be more **sustainable** and **fair.**"*
>
> *— Gordon Renouf, CEO of Good On You*

GREENPEACE DETOX (GLOBAL)

This **campaign** exposes the direct links between global clothing brands, their suppliers, and toxic water pollution around the world. Greenpeace is campaigning to **stop the fashion industry** from continuing to **poison our water** sources with hazardous and hormone disrupting chemicals.

I:CO® / I:COLLECT (GLOBAL)

A **global solutions provider** and innovator in the realm of collection, reuse, and recycling of used apparel and footwear. Through its global **retail take-back system** and worldwide infrastructure, I:CO aims to help create a circular economy in the fashion industry.

↻ **Yay! You can find I:CO clothing recycle bins in malls and at BtL events around the world.**

MARSHALL DESIGN LA (L.A.)

MDLA consults fashion brands a for a more sustainable and cost effective alternative that empowers their clients to make the best decisions that meet their goals by providing access to cutting edge design, low impact materials, production methods, and fulfillment that will ripple well beyond a niche market, to become the standard, not the alternative.

NATURAL RESOURCES DEFENSE COUNCIL (U.S.)

Clean by Design is an **innovative program created by the NRDC** that uses the buying power of multinational corporations as leverage to reduce the environmental impacts of their suppliers abroad. Clean by Design focuses on improving process efficiency to reduce waste, emissions and improve the environment.

NOT JUST THE LABEL (LONDON & GLOBAL)

Not Just the Label is the world's leading **designer platform** for showcasing and nurturing today's pioneers in contemporary fashion.

ORGANIC COTTON ACCELERATOR PROGRAM
(THE NETHERLANDS)

OCA is an **accelerator program** that informs consumers and designers about cotton. Organic cotton is central to the fashion industry's transition to sustainability. The organic crop sets itself apart as a more sustainable alternative to growing cotton conventionally by vastly reducing the harmful effects of conventional production. Grown organically, cotton can benefit farmers and the environment alike, while meeting the growing market demand for sustainable clothing.

↻ **Yay! OCA has also partnered with Kering, as well as H&M, C&A, Eileen Fisher, and Textile Exchange.**

POST-LANDFILL ACTION NETWORK (U.S. & CANADA)

Post-Landfill Action Network (also known as, the PLAN) cultivates, educates, and inspires the **student-led zero waste movement.** We inform students about the waste crisis and equip them with the necessary skills and resources to implement solutions to waste in their campus communities. PLAN empowers our generation to be changemakers.

↻ **Yay! The list of colleges that participate is ever growing and encouraging that aspirational informed shoppers are taking over the world.**

QUEEEN OF RAW (N.Y.C.)

A **marketplace connecting designers** looking for quick and easy access to affordable fabrics with low minimums from the manufacturers currently sitting on $100B worth of quality excess stock.

RED CARPET GREEN DRESS (L.A., GLOBAL)

This is where positive fashion meets the red carpet. Inspired by the global red carpet opportunity presented by husband James Cameron's blockbuster hit 'Avatar' in 2009, Suzy Amis Cameron founded a unique and innovative dress design contest called 'Red Carpet Green Dress'. Now going into its ninth year, the **positive fashion campaign** sets the challenge for creatives, emerging and established designers worldwide to create a Red Carpet worthy dress, or tuxedo, from environmentally and socially responsible fabrics – thus fulfilling the Green Dress criteria. The final ethical design will be worn on the red carpet at the Annual Academy Awards® on 4th March 2018. (Dresses worn by: Emma Roberts, Gina Rodriguez, Missi Pyle, Naomi Harris. Tux worn by: Kellan Lutz)

↻ **Yay! Red Carpet Green Dress + Reformation = "No Red Carpet Needed" Line of Eco-Dresses. Launched at the annual RCGD Oscar party. Styled by none other than Taryn, who paired the gorgeous dresses with vegan shoes.**

REDRESS ASIA / ECOCHIC DESIGN AWARD / BYT (GLOBAL)

ReDress is an **environmental non-governmental organization (NGO)** working to reduce waste in the fashion industry and organizes the EcoChic Design Award, a sustainable fashion design competition, which inspires emerging designers to create mainstream clothing with minimal textile waste.

↻ **Yay! The first winner of the EcoChic Design Award will receive an offer to design an upcycled collection on BYT's forthcoming e-commerce platform and at Lane Crawford, Asia's leading luxury department store. BYT is a new affordable luxury, upcycled fashion brand with ambitious plans for its commitment to sustainability – including upcycling excess garments, working with Asia's top sustainable manufacturing facilities, and using the most innovative sustainable processes available.**

SUUCHI INC. (NEW JERSEY)

Suuchi Ramesh founded Suuchi Inc. 3 years ago after a 10-year career in technology and predictive data analytics. Suuchi Inc is a next generation supply chain technology platform that manufactures apparel and accessories for brands of all sizes. In 3 years, the company is 140+ employees and 200 customers and growing. The company's hyper-growth has been possible through the development and use of Suuchi's innovative PLM software and app, the Suuchi Grid. This platform provides hundreds of companies access to a transparent supply chain and data to make smart decisions for their brand. Our team is 60% women who come from 20+ nationalities and 5 generations. Through our training and education programs, we are able to certify women in Hudson County and empower them to re-enter the workforce.

SUSTAINABLE APPAREL COALITION / HIGG INDEX (S.F. / GLOBAL)

The Coalition's vision is for apparel, footwear, and textiles industries to no longer fuel unnecessary environmental harm and yield a positive impact on the people and communities associated with its activities. The **Higg Index** is an **apparel and footwear industry self-assessment standard** for measuring environmental and social sustainability throughout the supply chain.

THE RENEWAL WORKSHOP (OREGON)

This **sustainably-minded company** partners with the world's most popular brands and retailers to renew their "unsellable" returns and excess inventory. In its Portland-based facility, each garment reemerges as Renewed Apparel through their proprietary processes, which is then either sold back to the brand through their sales channels, or The Renewal Workshop sells the product through its own retailer network. For any product that cannot be renewed, the Workshop responsibly oversees its upcycling, downcycling, or recycling in order to optimize its materials.

○ **Yay! Brands like Toad & Co, prAna, Mountain Khakis, and Ibex are partnered with The Renewal Workshop.**

TRASH-2-CASH (U.K.)

A European Union funded **research project aiming to create regenerated fibers** from pre-consumer and post-consumer waste. It's also pioneering an entirely new way of developing materials by utilizing zero-value waste textiles and fibers with design driven technologies to create high quality products.

MORE TO COME:

Balanced Fashion

Federal Trade Association

GFX (Global Fashion Exchange)

Greenpeace MAKE SMTHNG Week #Makechangenow

LACI (Los Angeles Cleantech Incubator)

↻ **Yay! Thought leaders are gathering to get Textile Recycling up and running in Los Angeles.**

Mochni

Native Styling

NPD

P.A.S.S. (Product and Social Safety)

Plug and Play Ventures

Pollima - A society that upcycles, recycles, and uses waste as sustenance.

REMODE - THE PREMIERE EVENT FOR DISRUPTIVE AND SUSTAINABLE FASHION

Sustainable Brands

TB/AC (The Button / Accessory Connection) - GOTS Certified

↻ **Yay! They've got GOTS Certified Zippers. Look for pics of 3 awesome jackets and the sentence "Show stopper pieces from The 2nd Annual Beyond the Label Fashion Show + Tell Concert Couture jackets" to check the GOTS Certified Zippers out.**

The Full Edit

The Future of Fashion

The Library - Study Hall Conferences

The Psychology of Fashion

The RealReal

Worn Again Technologies

Incredible panel breaking it down!

Sold out - and then some!

Gina Garcia empowers!

Triarchy Denim

Bead & Reel

**Concert Couture
Beyond the Label - SMC**

With sincere gratitude to The City of Santa Monica, Sustainable Works & Santa Monica College.

Photos by: Janell Hipwell Photography

Industry of All Nations

Buffalo Exchange

Chop Shop Fashion - SMC

Tradesy

Healthier Fashion Industry Cohorts

*This list includes **organizations** that may not focus on sustainable fashion, but do support important **issues related** to the current state of the **fashion industry**.*

- **Broccoli City:** A non-profit which hosts Broccoli City Festival (BC Fest) to shift youth's relationship to sustainability via hip-hop, yoga, healthy food, and healthy fashion

- **Dress for Success:** An organization that gifts women in need with secondhand professional clothes for job interviews and so much more

- **Environmental Media Association Awards:** An organization that is considered the "eco-Oscars" for film and television; this award show spotlights TV shows, TV episodes, and films that promote environmental stewardship

- **EPA (Environmental Protection Agency):** A federal agency that protects human health and the environment

- **Fashion Group International (FGI):** An organization that provides insights into major trends in the industry

- **Le Souk:** An online trade show featuring sustainable fabric options

- **Los Angeles International Textile Show (LA TEXTILE):** A textile tradeshow which is the fashion industry's premier West Coast textile, design, and production resource

- **SOURCING at MAGIC:** The world's largest fashion trade show for designers to source fabrics and trims

- **Natural Products Expo West:** A trade show for natural products, including sourcing for healthier laundry detergent, beauty care, and condoms

- **One Billion Rising:** A global movement started in 2012 to end violence against women, including sweatshop workers

- **Sustainable Works:** An environmental education and action-oriented organization

- **The Green Living Guy:** Seth Leitman is the go to guy for environmental vehicle technology information among many other industries and a big BtL supporter.

Yay! BtL partnered with Sustainable Works, Santa Monica College, and the city of Santa Monica to launch the Beyond the Label Fashion Show + Tell.

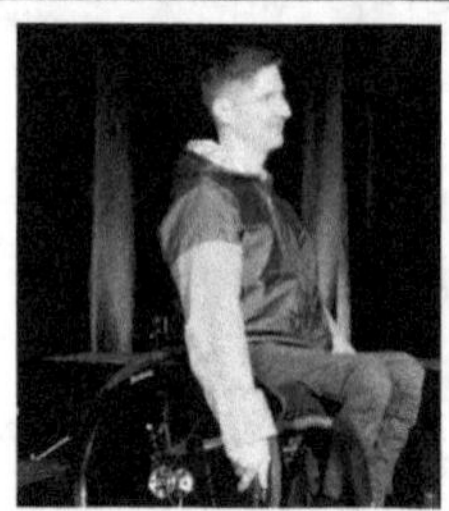

Show stopper pieces from **The 2nd Annual Beyond the Label Fashion Show + Tell. Concert Couture** jackets worn by Infinite Flow dancer Marc Lafleur, super star SMC student model, and super rad BtL team member Allison Sherman. Jackets created in an experimental class in partnership with Beyond the Label at Santa Monica College. Students learned to repurpose tents left behind at music festivals.

EcoDivas + TedxLA = Beyond the Label: Taryn is wearing her PERI repurposed butterfly skirt, organic cotton BtL tee by Metawear, and Fahima wrist cuff alongside the super awesome nerdtastic BtL team of superstars at the TedxLA City Experiment - The BtL T-Shirt Exchange at the Skirball Cultural Center.

○ **TEDxLA:** TEDx is designed to help communities, organizations, and individuals spark conversation and connection through local TED-like experiences.

○ **Texworld USA:** An international business platform and can't-miss industry event that showcases new innovations and sustainable fabric & trim options.

○ **The Story of Stuff Project:** The original video, "The Story of Stuff," from Annie Leonard, explains the concept of controlled obsolescence in production, including fashion.

○ **Turning Green:** A global student-led movement promoting healthy fashion and beauty choices

○ **Waste and Resource Action Programme (WRAP):** A program for resource efficiency experts

GET YOUR NERD ON!

We've included a list of additional resources and mind-blowing, mindful content to educate, inform, and inspire you to #MakeShiftHappen

● **Beyond the Label (YouTube)** - A short video that honestly answers the question: What the 'f' is in our clothes? and empowers shoppers to #MakeShiftHappen

● **"Clean Clothes Project 2016/Industry of All Nations"** (Vimeo): This video introduces you to loomed organic cotton in India, which is dyed by passionate workers using native all-natural dyes.

● **"Clothes to Die for"** (BBC documentary): The dark reality of the third-world garment industries has been revealed in programmes such as Blood, Sweat and T-Shirts (BBC) or ITV's Fashion Factories Undercover. Few, however, have been as powerful as tonight's documentary. Director Zara Hayes is careful to consider the context of the tragedy.

- **"Greenpeace - Detox Fashion"** (YouTube): This animated, Hunger Games-esque video exposes you to unregulated dye and chemical dumping, fast fashion and planned obsolescence.

- **"Fashion: Last Week Tonight with John Oliver"** (HBO/YouTube): This brilliant piece of British humor-tinged news covers Toxic Fast Fashion 101.

- **Handprint** (EcoAge TV/YouTube): This video offers an intimate look at the creation of a garment and all the hands required to bring it into the world.

- **If Selena Gomez's song "Bad Liar" Was About Sustainable Shopping from Global Citizen** (Facebook): This solution-based spoof is a fun and sexy romp for socially conscious shoppers.

- **Lenzing & Recover** (LABeyondtheLabel.com): These short videos show how to recycle waste fabric into new fabric, as well as the process behind making eucalyptus fabric. Nerd alert!

- **Krochet Kids** (Kickstarter): This hugely successful crowdfunding campaign introduces super cute, ethically-made hats and the people that make them.

- **1 Million Women - Microfiber pollution** (Facebook): This short video shares horrific facts about microfibers and how you can be more responsible.

- **Next level eco fashion! - Kiss The Ground** (YouTube): This quirky short video documents traditional fabric making skills being revitalized to make quality goods that don't harm our soil.

  ○ **Yay! Keep an eye out in 2018 for the *Kiss the Ground* documentary by award-winning filmmakers Josh and Rebecca Tickell of Big Picture Ranch. *Kiss The Ground* works to restore soils worldwide by promoting and developing models that accelerate the adoption of regenerative agriculture.**

- **PACT Organic: Change You Can Wear, How Much Did Your Underwear Cost? And 5 Reasons To Change Your Clothes Timelapse** (YouTube): These commercials market to shoppers who care about innovative supply chain solutions and positive impactful retail options.

- *RiverBlue* - This documentary film exposes unregulated dumping, dead rivers with no fish, and people still bathing in and drinking from toxic water sources.

- **Sweatshop - Deadly Fashion** (YouTube): This heart-wrenching mini-series gives you a look inside unethical fast fashion production seen through the eyes of young fashionistas/os that buy the clothes. (Have tissues ready.)

- *The True Cost* (Netflix and iTunes): This must-see documentary exposes the entire fashion supply chain's dark secrets. You cannot unsee this film.

- **The woman who wants you to rent used baby clothes** (BBC News): This positive, solution-based news piece introduces a fashion business that reduces waste and helps moms do good.

- **This clothing line is saving its waste and paying fair wages** (via Zero Waste Daniel on Facebook): This video is about a solution-based clothing line saving its waste, paying its workers a fair wage, and creating picturesque works of art.

- **Unacceptable Levels** (documentary): Our bodies are changing, as synthetic chemicals are becoming an everyday experience for all of us.

- **Walmart The High Cost Of Low Price** (YouTube): This documentary introduces you to all aspects of a big-box store's supply chain, retail, and marketing, and how they impact local economies and waste global resources. (Some shift has taken place at Walmart since this documentary launched over a decade ago, but we hope that they do more.)

---

*"In the course of researching, I came across an article that showed a Google Maps image of a **river in China** that flowed into a bay supplying water to Hong Kong, and millions of people. The **river** had a large streak of **indigo blue** you could literally see from outer space. The **pollution** was coming from an area that billed itself as the **"blue jeans capital of the world"** due to the amount of jeans they manufacture – **200 million pairs annually** from **60 different brands**, which are then sent to North America. I also discovered that nine billion pairs of jeans are made every year, and in a very toxic way. For me, I felt this distressing truth would make for a good story, one that had not been told to date."*

– David McIlvride, writer and director of the RiverBlue documentary

> *"When you go to these places – the factories in* **China, Bangladesh, and India** *– the smell of the chemicals is really impactful. The* **chemicals burn** *your eyes. That's something no amount of research could have taught us. To experience what these people are living and working in daily was heartbreaking, and to know and see these chemicals in their drinking water – it's completely* **unacceptable."**
>
> *– Roger Williams, producer and co-director of RiverBlue*

EDUCATING THE NEXT GENERATION

- **BFDA**
- **C.L.A.S.S.**
- **Concert Couture Class** - Santa Monica College
- **Global Fashion Management School of Graduate Studies** - FIT (Fashion Institute of Technology)
- **Specialized Studios** - Parsons

SUSTAINABLE FASHION STUDENT GROUPS EMERGING AMONGST DESIGNERS AND NON-DESIGNERS:

- **Mentorship Program for students/recent graduates** - Beyond the Label
- **Chop Shop** - Santa Monica College
- **FAST** - UCLA
- **Oikos** - Parsons
- **UNRAVEL** - UCLA

CHAPTER 6:

Who Are You Wearing?
*Unique **style profiles** from **industry insiders** and what they give a shift about*

"Choosing **'knowledge is power'** over **'ignorance is bliss'** is how we **#MakeShiftHappen"** - Taryn Hipwell

Just what *is* sustainable fashion? We find it easiest to break this explanation down into five categories:

People shop in different ways, so where do you fall?

ETHICAL FASHION

Fair trade, fair treatment for every worker in every step of the supply chain

CLEAN (HEALTHY) FASHION

Biodegradable, natural, and non-toxic dyes and fibers that are skin-friendly

LOCAL FASHION

Crafty brands and artisans that sell items produced locally

RECYCLED FASHION

Fabric and clothes that are reused, recycled, repurposed, or upcycled to reduce waste

VEGAN FASHION

Clothing produced with zero animal products

Top Chefs
(AKA our style mavens) and their specialties

We asked some of our favorite stylish people around the industry to divulge the **eco-friendly** rationale behind their **shopping habits.**

1. **Alicia Carrasco** - Journalist, educator, Fashion Revolution Ambassador, and #ShopLocal advocate

2. **Ashley Frohnert** - Cruelty-free activist and The Happy Veganista fashion blogger

3. **Benita Robeldo** - Actress, director, Compassion Fashion: Clothes (with Benita Robledo) vlogger

4. **Bianca Alexander** - Creative director and host of Conscious Living TV, Fashion Revolution Ambassador

5. **Daniel Silverstein "Zero Waste Daniel"** - New York based clothing designer and zero waste pioneer

6. **Jeanelly Concepcion** - Style Blogger

7. **Joshua Katcher** - Vegan menswear designer and The Discerning Brute blogger

8. **Karen Housel** - Environmental scientist and founder of Sustainable Daisy fashion blog

9. **Kathryn Knox** - Founder of Stone Sevyn, event and fashion show producer, stylist and consultant for sustainable luxury and fashion

10. **Taryn Hipwell** - Founder of Beyond the Label

The TOP CHEF approach:

- **Recipe (For Success):** How to create a great look
- **~~Diet~~ Lifestyle for Shift Shopping:** How they shifted their shopping habits and why
- **Shift Shopping List:** What, why, and who they shop for
- **Stocked Pantry:** What you'll find in their closet

A *WORD OF ADVICE* FROM SOME OF OUR FAVORITE BLOGGERS:

" *Honestly, I'm not the kind of woman who could only buy what she "needs." I love beautiful things, I love feeling put together and current. But I **never shop for fun, as a social activity, or to pass the time.** When I want something, I put it on a list and wait for a while to see if I truly want it, and that it isn't an impulse purchase. **Trends come and go.** If I do find that I still want something, I use the shopping guide on EcoCult.com – **'Where to Find Sustainable Fashion'** – and try to find a version online that uses sustainable materials and was made by **fairly-paid labor.** If I want something fun, trendy, or cheap, or I need it immediately, I go to a secondhand shop to pick it up there.* "

– Alden Wicker, founder of N.Y.C. sustainable fashion blog, EcoCult

" *I am a practicing **minimalist** and because of this, my relationship to fashion is different. I don't have 'flings' with fashion items and, for me, **impulse shopping** is a thing of the past. Since my sustainable fashion awakening in 2008, I have tried to **live an intentional life** which means being conscious in my decisions and extends to my shopping choices. When an item is brought into my home, it is because it fills a need or I truly love it. **Waste is unsustainable**. Here's the process I follow before buying something: First, I ask myself, **'Do I need it?'** If yes, then I ask myself, **'Can I find it secondhand within the time frame allowed?'** If so, I'll start searching websites such as eBay and Gumtree or go op-shopping. If I need the item immediately, I always do research so I can find out: What's the piece made from and is it **sustainable?** Was it **ethically made? Who made it?** Is it **built to last?** What is the **reputation of the company** or business I'm purchasing from? Is it **within my budget?** The answers to these questions are then weighed and I make the best choice from the available options. It's taken me years to get to this point, so I don't expect people to change their shopping behaviors overnight. We are hard wired from a young age to **consume mindlessly** and feed our consumer addictions with things. But if you make a concerted effort each day to ask yourself the above questions, you'll find these habits become second nature and your relationship to stuff will transform. **It's about progress, not perfection**, so as long as you keep trying to make better, more sustainable decisions, you're already doing better than most!* "

– Jennifer Nini, founder and editor of Eco Warrior Princess

TOP "LOCAL" CHEF

ALICIA CARRASCO

Journalist, educator, Fashion Revolution Ambassador, and #ShopLocal advocate

RECIPE (FOR SUCCESS)

1. Review Your Wardrobe
Before shopping I always review what's already in my closet so that I can avoid buying duplicate or similar garments or accessories.

2. Buy Locally
I always try to shop for garments that have been produced locally and are handmade because it's a wonderful, responsible way to contribute to and enrich the local economy.

3. Choose Secondhand Locally
I firmly believe there's nothing more sustainable than what already exists, so I love buying new clothes in secondhand and thrift stores. I always find excellent options without spending a lot of money.

4. Shop Your Values
Once or twice a year, I buy garments or accessories from sustainable brands. Before doing so, I always analyze their story, values, mission, and production methods to make sure I'm supporting a brand that believes in and practices sustainability.

"LOCAL" ~~DIET~~ LIFESTYLE FOR SHIFT SHOPPING

I made the decision to stop buying fast fashion in 2014. I vividly remember searching online for information about slow lifestyles and healthy food. When I came across a post on a Spanish blog, "Wellness Juice," talking about "the Fashion Revolution movement," it highlighted the tragedy of Rana Plaza, Bangladesh, where 1,134 people were killed and over 2,500 injured when the factory complex collapsed in April 2013. Most of the victims were working in extremely precarious situations, sewing clothes for big international fashion brands. After that, I looked for more information on the fast fashion industry and its social and environmental costs, realizing that, as much as I loved fashion, I didn't want to contribute to an industry that treated people like slaves in their supply chain, polluted thousands of rivers, slaughtered animals for their fur, and more. I found that it was possible to develop new habits as a more responsible consumer and make better shopping decisions.

SHIFT SHOPPING LIST

Secondhand, local, vegan, upcycled, eco-friendly, fair trade, handmade, well-tailored

STOCKED PANTRY

- **Outerwear:** Coat by Slow Artist. Organic cotton, ethically and locally made in Valencian Community, Spain

- **Shoes:** Wedge heels shoes by Slowers. Organic cotton GOTS Certified, handmade in Castellón Valencian Community, Spain

- **Bracelet:** Bracelets by Alex and Ani. Sustainable materials made in the U.S.

- **Necklace:** Upcycled necklace by Beatriz Constan. Recycled leather and handmade in Salobreña, Granada

- **Purse:** Denim clutch by Slow Artist. Organic cotton, ethically, and locally made in Valencian Community, Spain

TOP "CRUELTY-FREE" CHEF

ASHLEY FROHNERT

Cruelty-free activist and The Happy Veganista fashion blogger

RECIPE (FOR SUCCESS)

1. Seek Inspiration
Before shopping, I search for trendy items on Google, chat with coworkers about sustainable vegan brands we like, and keep an eye out on Instagram.

2. Follow Cruelty-Free Fashion Bloggers
I follow some general fashion bloggers as well as vegan or sustainable bloggers, like Fashion Veggie, so I gather ideas from their posts to inspire me while shopping.

3. Find Vegan Stores
I find most of my clothes at Silverlake Farmers Market in Los Angeles, local, vegan, or sustainable living events, thrift and vintage stores, vegan fashion websites, like Bead & Reel, or small boutiques.

4. Depop and Google Search "Cruelty-Free"
If I'm looking for a specific item that I haven't been able to find locally, I'll use Depop (a secondhand global marketplace) or Google to try to find it elsewhere.

5. Stay Away from Non-Vegan Options
I try to avoid the mall or anywhere that sells fast fashion, if I can. Stores in the mall generally don't have a large selection of sustainable clothing, plus, I'll admit that I can be easily tempted by all the unsustainable options.

"CRUELTY-FREE" ~~DIET~~ LIFESTYLE FOR SHIFT SHOPPING

I was vegetarian for about four years before going vegan. I committed to being fully cruelty-free in my eating habits, makeup, and wardrobe after reading the book Beg by Rory Freedman and learning that animals are abused and killed for leather, wool, angora, and down just as much as they are for meat, eggs, and dairy. My biggest advice is to have fun exploring all of the innovative ways people are creating animal-free materials! It's really exciting to increasingly watch companies find ways to make new cruelty-free textiles. There's really no new way to make fabric out of dead animals, but there are endless ways to build beautiful, innovative, cruelty-free materials.

SHIFT SHOPPING LIST

Vegan, ethically-made, fashionable, edgy and hip, durable, unique, supporting people, and causes I care about.

STOCKED PANTRY

- **Shirts:** Vegan Soup Warhol Art Shirt by Lef0u
- **Outerwear:** Patagonia Insulated Prairie Dawn Parka, made of 100% organic cotton canvas, lined with recycled polyester fleece in all but the sleeves (I ordered it online after seeing it on a PETA vegan coat list).
- **Shoes:** Vegan Leather Sinclairs by NICORA Shoes, made in L.A., and MooShoes my boyfriend got for me in Silverlake
- **Hats:** Dark green faux suede hat gifted to me for Christmas, it's Billabong.
- **Accessories/Bags:** Matt & Nat Brave Backpack in Chili, Matt & Nat Jorja Small Dwell Hobo bag. Both are made out of recycled water bottles.

TOP "GLOBAL CONNECTER" CHEF

BENITA ROBELDO

Actress, director, Compassion Fashion: Clothes (with Benita Robledo) vlogger

RECIPE (FOR SUCCESS)

1. **Follow Your Intuition**

For me clothing is all about expressing how I feel, which changes day to day, sometimes on the hour. I've been known to change multiple times a day, so when I'm putting an outfit together I just listen to how I feel: What piece of clothing makes me shout "Yes!" It tends to take longer this way and is certainly messier, but I can honestly say I love everything I own.

2. **Keep Your Standards High**

I don't necessarily follow trends, so I'm only an occasional shopper. I'll spend a few hours shopping online until I find just the right piece. And now that I've been shopping ethically for a few years, I have my go-to online retailers so it doesn't take as long.

3. **Check Out High-Quality Ethical Fashion Blogs**

One of my favorite places to learn about brands and ethical textiles is the Bead & Reel blog. It's always informative and fun. I also have several friends who work in the ethical fashion space, so I'm lucky that they always share their discoveries with me.

"GLOBAL CONNECTER" ~~DIET~~ LIFESTYLE FOR SHIFT SHOPPING

Five years ago, I went to a local craft exhibition and met the owners of Raven + Lily. I loved their jewelry, but was most struck by the story of the women who made jewelry. It was like a light bulb went off in my head. I had no idea that you could shop and make the world a better place at the same time. I'd always done my best to buy organic and local, but I didn't know I could extend this conscientiousness to fashion. It was a powerful moment.

SHIFT SHOPPING LIST

It's hard to find things that check every box, so I look for pieces that check at least three of my criteria: Does it give back in some way? Is it vegan? Does it help the environment? Does it have a low environmental impact? Is it organic? Is it made with fair labor practices? Is it vintage? Is it repurposing a material that would normally go to waste?

STOCKED PANTRY

- ○ **Leggings:** Smoke Aluminum leggings from Nuvango
- ○ **Socks:** Banned books socks from Out of Print Clothing
- ○ **Undergarments:** Anything by Naja
- ○ **Glasses:** Valencia sunglasses by Wear Panda
- ○ **Accessories:** Half-moon earrings from Canned Goods Co.

TOP "LOW IMPACT" CHEF

BIANCA ALEXANDER

Creative director and host of Conscious Living TV, Fashion Revolution Ambassador

RECIPE (FOR SUCCESS)

1. Treat Shopping Like a Treasure Hunt
Why deplete the earth's precious resources to make one more dress when there are literally millions of great ones out there in excellent condition looking for good homes? I love the thrill of a treasure hunt.

2. Do Your Homework
I love blogs like The Notepasser and Ecocult, Conscious Chatter podcast, and the Ethical Writers Coalition (a group of journalists, writers and bloggers who seek to support and further ethical and sustainable living). I love watching all of our sustainable fashion content on the "Style Ethics" on Conscious Living TV.

3. Wear What Brings You Joy
In the spirit of Marie Kondo – author of cult favorite guide, "The Life-Changing Magic of Tidying Up" – my wardrobe is finely edited and curated. I know it intimately and only keep pieces that bring me joy and that I wear regularly.

4. Gently Used Clothes Are Your New Best Friend
My favorite vintage store is American Rag Cie. I scout the racks of the Hollywood Flea Market on Fairfax, or trade in some of my gently loved clothes for an upcycled new look from Crossroads or Buffalo Exchange.

5. Avoid Fast Fashion
I avoid anything made with artificial dyes and synthetic fabrics from big-box stores that fail to take into account the true cost of making a garment – be it human, environmental, or health-oriented.

"LOW IMPACT" ~~DIET~~ LIFESTYLE FOR SHIFT SHOPPING

In 2003, I went vegetarian for health, spiritual, and eventually humane and environmental reasons. However, it took me some time to translate those values to my wardrobe. In 2011, I went vegan after a 30-day detox eating only raw foods, and began exploring cruelty-free fashion. I thought it would be hard at first, but just like swapping meat and cheese with daiya or tempeh, I quickly realized that there are dozens of stylish alternatives for conscious fashionistas, like Cri de Coeur, Vaute and Olsenhaus, among others.

When it comes to personal style, I consider myself an artist. My body is the canvas, and fashion is my paint. Color is everything. In Bali, where I currently live, they even assign a different color to each day of the week!

SHIFT SHOPPING LIST

Natural fabric and dyes, ethically-made, vegan, great fit, made to last

STOCKED PANTRY

- ○ **Outerwear:** Vaute - Vegan, fair trade winter and raincoats, Made in N.Y.C. and Buffalo Exchange - Vaute Vintage faux leather Moto Jackets
- ○ **Pants/Shorts:** Shining Shakti tie-dye Yoga Pants, organic, fair trade, woman owned, Made in Virginia
- ○ **Shoes:** Mohop Shoes, FSC Certified Wood tie-on sandals (with changeable ribbons!)
- ○ **Glasses/Sunglasses:** Eynack, made from Bamboo and various vintage styles
- ○ **Accessories:** Vintage Straw Sunhat (I currently live in Bali!) and Natural Mala Bead Necklaces, blessed by Self-Realization Fellowship Monastics

TOP "ZERO WASTE" CHEF

"ZERO WASTE DANIEL" *(Daniel Silverstein)*

New York based clothing designer and zero waste pioneer

RECIPE (FOR SUCCESS)

1. Comfort
I really just try to think about what I actually want and what makes me feel comfortable.

2. Capsule Challenge
I recently did a capsule challenge, where I only wore nine items for a week. I didn't need more than nine items of clothing to be comfortable, to get work done, to be professional, to be able to move or to be stylish.

3. Research Before Purchase
I do a lot of research into a brand before I buy from them to make sure they are not only using natural or recycled fiber, but also making their products in ethical conditions and paying their workers a fair wage. My favorite videos for inspiration are: Read Li Edelkoort's anti-fashion manifesto. Watch Annie Leonard's talk (at The New School) on zero waste design and justice.

4. **I mostly wear my own clothes, but I shop at other ethical clothing companies like Brave GentleMan, which makes vegan clothing, and Everlane, which also sources natural materials and is transparent.**

The ZWD team visits local factories and collects textile scraps left behind from the textile cutting process. All those beautiful textiles cost factory owners money to cart off to landfill. Instead we take as much of it as we can and bring it back to our make/shop where it gets sewn into our one of a kind reroll. Normally when you cut patterns with a marker in traditional fashion you will waste 15% to 20% of the material that is cut and goes straight into landfills and is scrapped. So all of our patterns put together make some jigsaw puzzles, so that this is eliminated or brought down to less than 1%. We draw a lot of our inspiration from the styles of New York City and try to capture the fun and funk of street fashion while also designing beyond the gender binary.

"Zero Waste" ~~DIET~~ LIFESTYLE FOR SHIFT SHOPPING

I've always been an advocate for environmental causes and studied Natural Resource I studied at FIT and the training and exposure I got to the industry there and at the sister school, Politecnico di Milano, Italy, encouraged me to incorporate sustainable practices into my business. And just as a member of youth culture it's a very important thing to be concerned about the future of our planet, so also when I think about employing people and truly being innovative as a designer, what I want to bring is not just a sense of style, but a way of making things that are better for us. I like to make things, to solve problems, and to look and feel good doing it. I wanted to prove that beauty and responsible consumption could co-exist, merging my passions. I emulated my mentors and idols, but was an advocate that fashion had a new direction to move in, one that could value rooted things in the earth, the air we breathe, our real bodies, but still nourish our eyes with glamor and fill hearts with wonder. My hope was that the world would make a little space and I could follow in the footsteps of the greats, selling to the top stores, leaving a legacy of beautiful

work, but with the current eye of a global environmentalist. I grew up in a household that always stressed recycling so I naturally had an interest in sustainability. In college, as an intern in the industry and at my first job out of college, I was able to see firsthand just how much material is discarded in fashion production and this shifted my way of thinking to pursuing zero waste as a designer. As I grew, I began to implement zero waste in other aspects of my everyday life because it only felt right to minimize my waste footprint in all aspects of my life. At work we encourage everyone at the office to recycle, we use left-over materials for other projects, we donate scraps to an artist who works only with textiles, and our interns run all around the fashion district with tote bags, no plastic bags from my office!

Recycle your old garments. There are several recycling facilities (like the North Face, H&M and Greenmarket Clothing Collection) where you can bring your old clothes, even if they have stains or rips.

Look for clothes made of natural fibers like organic cotton rather than synthetic fibers like polyester, which can take over 200 years to decompose.

I live my whole life, not just my clothing, without waste. Food packaging and food waste are huge contributors to our daily trash production (4.4lbs per person every day!!). Shop locally, bring your own containers, and buy in bulk. Look at your life and see where you can best eliminate waste.

You CAN make a difference, just by changing the way you think, the way you buy, and the way you look at your own waste habits. Even small change is good change.

SHIFT SHOPPING LIST

Made of natural or recycled fiber, produced domestically, little to no packaging, transparency about who made the clothes, comfort

STOCKED PANTRY

- **Pants/Outerwear/Knits/Bags:** ZWD joggers / ZWD jean jacket / ZWD mock turtleneck / ZWD Essentials Pouch (all ZWD textiles are sourced from Brooklyn and handmade in our make/shop)

- **Undergarments:** BGreen underwear - made of organic cotton (non-toxic, no GMO), post-consumer recycled cotton, modal and TENCEL™ made in Dominguez, California

- **Shoes:** Z Shoes - 100% organic, sustainably harvested cotton from the Solo y San Miguel regions of Peru, 100% organic plant dyes, soles made with sustainably-harvested Amazonian Sharinga rubber

- **Glasses/Sunglasses:** Proof Eyewear - made from sustainable materials including FSC-certified wood, cotton-based acetate, and repurposed skateboard decks

TOP "SHOP YOUR CLOSET" CHEF

Style Blogger

RECIPE (FOR SUCCESS)

1. Need vs. Whim
I rarely shop for something on a whim. I have to have the need for something new or for a specific event, trip, or episode filming.

2. Shop my Closet
When I'm putting outfits together to film for my shows on Style Lush TV, take photos for my blog, or for events, I definitely shop my closet first.

3. Shop for Longevity
Over the years, I've definitely accumulated plenty of clothing between classic pieces and trendier items. I tend to buy more of the classic or timeless styles so I can reuse and restyle many times over.

4. Pick Your Pleasure
As an artist, one of the ways I enjoy expressing myself is through an outfit. My looks usually reflect my current inspiration and express a specific mood.

5. Meant for Me
If I don't need anything, but I see something I love, I might try it on, but I convince myself that I don't need it or I'll leave it and if I come back and it's still available then I get it because it was "meant for me".

"SHOP YOUR CLOSET" ~~DIET~~ LIFESTYLE FOR SHIFT SHOPPING

Conservation and Management - I've always been huge on Reduce, Reusing and Recycling but it was only in the last 5 years that I became aware of how harmful the fashion industry can be. From production to packaging, I now look for clothing that has the least amount of impact on the environment. I think my biggest tip is to read the labels, look for ethically sourced materials, fair-trade if possible and sustainably produced.

Shop your closet! Sometimes I'll pull out a dress that I haven't worn in years and I'll restyle it with a belt, different earrings, a new pair of shoes and/or handbag. You can even do your hair in a different way and the look is completely new! Thrift shopping is awesome, too. I thrift online with Threadflip and Poshmark where I buy and sell lightly or brand new clothing. Less waste and it's like shopping a friend's closet! I have definitely found some amazing pieces, and thought, "How can anybody give this away?" I also recently discovered a boutique in the city (San Antonio) that does upcycling, and turns old or vintage pieces into something new and it's always so cool!

SHIFT SHOPPING LIST

Vegan for handbags & shoes, ethically made, stylish, affordable, fair trade

STOCKED PANTRY

- ○ **Shirts:** T-Shirt screen printed by Fashion Design students at International School of Design of the University of Turabo, Puerto Rico for Project "Hilo a Hilo" Thread by Thread. (As seen in photo)
- ○ **Pants/Shorts:** Vintage Guess Jeans, personal collection, 15 years old (As seen in photo)
- ○ **Undergarments & Socks:** MeUndies, Azura Bay (multiple brands), and EcoSox
- ○ **Hats:** Handmade from Puerto Rico
- ○ **Accessories/Bags:** Matt & Nat Handbags, Cult Gaia, Village Artisan Accessories

TOP "VEGAN" CHEF

JOSHUA KATCHER

Vegan menswear designer and The Discerning Brute blogger

RECIPE (FOR SUCCESS)

1. Investigate Your Options
Typically, I like to find a few brands that I really want to support, whose products I love. Once I put in the time to research, it's easy to find brands with values I stand behind.

2. Save Money to Support Success
Because ethical fashion tends to be a bit pricier, I buy the majority of my clothing from secondhand stores, so I can invest in brands that I really want to succeed.

3. Fashion Investment
It's important for people to view their fashion purchases as investments. If we want to see more sustainable, vegan materials, fair labor, and innovations, we really have to invest in the things we buy.

4. Build It with Layers
Aesthetically speaking, I really like classy menswear with a modern twist. Often my perfect outfit starts with deciding on my pants, and then I build it out from there. I also like to layer, so usually I'll have a shirt and jacket, especially my Brave GentleMan moto jacket.

5. Be the Cruelty-Free Change You Wish to See
If we continue supporting brands that exploit workers, use cheap, crappy materials, and harm animals, then that's how things are going to continue to be made.

"VEGAN" ~~DIET~~ LIFESTYLE FOR SHIFT SHOPPING

I think having a vegan wardrobe makes just as much sense as having a vegan lifestyle. Unfortunately, there's a mainstream perception that food systems are more important than fashion and materials systems. People might be startled to find out, for example, that leather represents the most profitable aspect of the slaughter business, not meat. So leather isn't a byproduct at all. It's a meat subsidy.

In regards to shopping for shift, I'd simply recommend that people investigate what animals experience in the fashion production system. Look at the investigations into fur farms, angora farms, industrial shearing facilities, ostrich farms, crocodile farms, and slaughterhouses. If this is something that disturbs you, maybe it's time to consider no longer supporting these activities by buying products of cruelty.

SHIFT SHOPPING LIST

Well-designed, vegan, made fairly, organic, recycled or otherwise sustainable materials, secondhand, but no animals' hair or skin

STOCKED PANTRY

- ○ **Shirts:** Brave GentleMan Armor gray/black shirt
- ○ **Knits:** Vaute chunky-knit recycled cotton sweater
- ○ **Undergarments:** Hemen Biarritz organic cotton boxer briefs
- ○ **Pants/Shorts:** Brave GentleMan future-wool tweed pants
- ○ **Socks:** Zkano organic cotton gray socks
- ○ **Glasses/Sunglasses:** Modo Eco recycled Dubai

TOP "SUSTAINABLE" CHEF

KAREN HOUSEL

Environmental scientist, founder of Sustainable Daisy fashion blog, and secondhand style maven

RECIPE (FOR SUCCESS)

1. Only Buy What You Love

I only buy things that I find to be truly useful. I've consciously turned down clothing that I 'sort of' like, because that's not enough for me to add it to my wardrobe. My closet is my sanctuary, and I only want beautifully-made, sustainable pieces to go in it!

2. Keep Tabs on Eco Bloggers

I follow a bunch of green lifestyle bloggers. One of my favorites is Jenn Im of Clothes Encounters, who frequently shares her thrift shop hauls. She has millions of fans, but still goes to Goodwill to snag vintage finds. I think that's so cool!

3. Thrift Shops Are Everything

I love to shop at thrift shops and vintage stores, and sometimes online. My favorite places are Crossroads Trading Co., The Closet, Council Thrift Shops, Hope of the Valley Thrift Store, Buffalo Exchange, and Goodwill. I also like shopping secondhand online, at sites like thredUP, Depop, and Rent the Runway.

4. Have an Open (Eco) Mind

When I walk into a thrift store, I have a very open mind. I'm always on the hunt for something great, but I don't get bothered if it doesn't work out on every visit.

5. Pick Natural Fiber and Avoid Synthetics

Recently, I've been avoiding polyester because I want to reduce my consumption of synthetics.

"SUSTAINABLE" ~~DIET~~ LIFESTYLE FOR SHIFT SHOPPING

I've always been a huge thrift shopper. I never felt like clothing had to be brand new to be stylish or more valuable. In my early 20's, I remember opening my closet and realizing that 80% of my clothing was worn before me, and I realized: "Wait, this is sustainable fashion!" I thought about how many resources and how much energy was saved just by wearing clothes that already existed in the world. After college I was itching for a hobby that could keep my spirits up in the wake of my job hunt. I was already interested in recycled fashion, so I looked online for sustainable fashion bloggers, but I couldn't find many who were writing in the colorful, guilt-free way that I wanted to read. I saw an opportunity. I figured if I wanted to follow a fun, funky green lifestyle blogger, others probably would too. That's the moment Sustainable Daisy blog was born!

SHIFT SHOPPING LIST

Sustainably-sourced materials, ethically-made, comfortable, and something I feel beautiful wearing!

STOCKED PANTRY

- ○ **Outerwear:** *A blue faux leather jacket I bought secondhand at a thrift store in Fukui, Japan for about $10*
- ○ **Long sleeve:** *A long sleeve floral top by Reformation that I bought secondhand from Crossroads Trading Co.*
- ○ **Skirt DIY:** *A maxi skirt with bright colorful prints of African animals. I cut it in half and adjusted the waist and made it into a mini skirt! The DIY was so easy, too!*
- ○ **Shirt:** *A funky purple flannel color-block piece from the Assistance League Thrift Store*
- ○ **Sunglasses:** *Gaia guy bamboo sunnies and hot pink shades from Buffalo Exchange*

TOP "LUXURY" CHEF

KATHRYN KNOX

Founder of Stone Sevyn, an environmentally conscious event production and consulting business

RECIPE (FOR SUCCESS)

1. Invest in Quality

I believe in quality over quantity and have a closet overflowing with beautiful clothes I've collected and curated over the years. These days I rarely purchase clothing unless I'm inspired by the story or see something truly unique. Specifically, I splurge on shoes, from brands like Stella McCartney. They're better quality, aren't made in countries with questionable human rights records and don't have a weird vegan shoe smell. For clothes, I buy new and from consignment shops, flea markets, and vintage stores.

2. Play With Color

I'm inspired by the color patterns in nature – bugs, forests, and flowers – and the way light reflects off the clouds when you're above them.

3. Pick What's (Almost) Perfect

There's a lot of judgment in the sustainable fashion space, with everyone expecting perfection. While we can all try, no company or person will ever be completely perfect when it comes to dressing both sustainably and fashionably. Still, I'm conscious of where my clothes are made, who makes it, what it's made of, and how it's made.

4. Embrace Authenticity

I was determined to inspire people to live more consciously and compassionately in a way that wasn't granola. When you live authentically, everything tends to work itself out.

"LUXURY" ~~DIET~~ LIFESTYLE FOR SHIFT SHOPPING

In 2000, I embraced sustainability into my lifestyle. It took me a few years to completely transition to a 100% plant-based diet and eliminate leather, but by 2006 I just couldn't fathom any other option, and I went "cold turkey" while vacationing in Sedona, Arizona. Back then sustainable fashion options were slim, but I was committed and I've never looked back.

SHIFT SHOPPING LIST

I ask myself: Where is it made? Who makes it? What is it made of? How is it made? Is it vegan?

STOCKED PANTRY

○ **Shirts:** *Coast / Made in Los Angeles*

○ **Knits & Shoes:** *Stella McCartney / Made in Italy*

○ **Jeans:** *Trave Denim / Made in Los Angeles*

○ **Swimwear:** *Cali Dreaming / Made in Los Angeles*

○ **Glasses:** *See Eyewear / Made in Germany*

TOP "ECODIVA" CHEF

TARYN HIPWELL

Founder of Beyond the Label

RECIPE (FOR SUCCESS)

1. **Shop for Free at Clothing Exchanges**
Save money, chill with friends, repeat seasonally!

2. **Shop for Cheap and Find Specific Items Secondhand**
Save money on previously sold pricey items and special items you need ASAP (Ex. I needed 4 1/2 inch heels to wear with your mom's fancy cruise dress to the Oscars. She's 2 inches taller than me. :) I found some beautiful pumps in a Los Feliz vintage shop).

3. **Self-Proclaimed Recycle-a-holic**
From secondhand clothing to up-cycled, repurposed, or recycled fabric (Love me some Recover, and some Refibra™ fibers from Lenzing), I prefer to reduce waste and chemical usage through my fashion purchases.

4. **Align with a brand's purpose, values, ethics, and for me, non-toxicity level.**
Seek out and support awesome designers who are passionate about like-minded issues! Spend your money on clothing items you fall in love with!

"ECODIVA" ~~DIET~~ LIFESTYLE FOR SHIFT SHOPPING

I expect (pleasantly push…that's my diva side that persists to persuade) transparency!

I create opportunities to meet many designers in person. I love to ask a lot of questions one on one. I prefer news directly from experts. This is why I also love to moderate panels and nerd out with a tribe of passionate people in the industry who intentionally #MakeShiftHappen.

When I learn about a new brand, I usually check their site for fabric information. If they don't have it listed, I call them for the details (if I'm feeling shy, I send an email!). Brands sharing resources and new technologies (Reformation, Patagonia, Eileen Fisher, Levi's) is rewarding for me, given that I got my start working for fashion designers in N.Y.C. that hid their resources.

SHIFT SHOPPING LIST

Am I going to be allergic to it? Is it made with toxic chemicals? Will microfibers harm the ocean? Does it harm the people that are making the product? Is the water unregulated in the area where it was made? If it's secondhand - is it a natural fiber? Does it need to be dry-cleaned or can it be washed and steamed out? EVERYONE SHOULD HAVE A STEAMER (they save time, money, and chemicals).

Do I love the story behind it when I hold it up and decide to wear it? When I applied for college, my art teacher Rettinger's recommendation letter shared that I dress my personality for the day. That habit got me into a great college and still serves me well today. Yay! And my clothes vary greatly to suit my being, while caring for other beings.

STOCKED PANTRY

- ○ **Shirts:**
    - Beyond the Label/MetaWear Organic Cotton/Seaweed Dye "Nutrition Label" tee
    - Beyond the Label/LA Relaxed Recover Fabric "Nutrition Label" tee
    - Beyond the Label/LA Relaxed TENCEL™ "Comical Care Label" tee
- ○ **Tank Top:** Groceries Apparel hemp black racerback and organic cotton pink tank
- ○ **Dress:** Reformation velvet deadstock ankle length dress, which I often shorten by ruching with safety pins on the sides
- ○ **Socks:** Organic Cotton PACT socks gifted by EcoDivas LLC (pre-Beyond the Label) at the *"EcoDivas / Fashion Revolution" Shorts & Sizzles Fest in 2014!*
- ○ **Accessories:** Chikumbuso crocheted plastic bag purse and Zambian magazine bead necklace and PACT, Boody, and AmaElla undies.

Yay! AmaElla recently launched the super cute, really well fitting "Romance" organic cotton undies line. Great for girlies that want to feel sexy (and have sensitive lady parts.)

*"I am always so **grateful** that people are open to hearing about all the "F"ed stuff in the **fashion industry** and even more grateful to share all the **new innovations** that incredible people are creating! It really does take each of us doing a little something to make a **huge impact**. Seriously, just by switching your T-shirt brand, not only could you be **saving a life**, but you could also be investing in the colorful life of a **healthy human living and working** in a **toxic free environment**. Is there a word more grateful than grateful? Because if there is I am that right now!"*

— Taryn Hipwell, founder of Beyond the Label

WWD

The NPD Group's chief industry adviser Marshall Cohen led the discussion about how companies and consumers can be more environmentally minded in their purchases and practices. Other participants included Taryn Hipwell, founder of Beyond the Label and author of "How to Shop for Shi(f)t"; Vanessa Urenda, cofounder of LAMINI; Valérie Martin, vice president of global communications and culture at the Aldo Group, and Sabra Krock creative director and co-owner of Everything but Water.

MEDIUM

Conscious Consumerism in Fashion - How you can Contribute to the Shift in the Industry Patrick Duffy, Founder of Global Fashion Exchange & Intandem Creatives, Anabel Maldonado, Founder of The Psychology of Fashion, Tara St James, Founder of Study N.Y. and Production Coordinator at Brooklyn Fashion + Design Accelerator, Taryn Hipwell, the founder of Beyond the Label, the author of *How to Shop for Shi(f) t*, Lauren Engelke, Sustainable Fashion Stylist and moderator, Nataliya Makulova, Founder of Balanced Fashion, Conscious Fashion Tech Consultant.

ETHICAL STYLE JOURNAL

How to Shop for Shi(f)t Feature in Issue 5

WE CANNOT CONTAIN OUR EXCITEMENT!

CHECK OUT THE NEXT BTL
SHOPPING GUIDE FOR DESIGNERS

We'll break down just what your money pays for when you shop, and how you can continue to #MakeShiftHappen to ensure a healthy local and global fashion industry.

FASHION-FORWARD VOCABULARY FOR THE ECO CURIOUS

*How many times have your eyes glazed over when you read the terms "fair trade," "vegan," or "circular economy?" We get it, ours have too, which is why we created **conversational definitions** that don't sound like they come from talking heads.*

Antimicrobial: Not stinky! Bacteria repellers. When you wear synthetics and exercise, and your armpits begin to sweat and stink, it's anti-microbial fabrics that help to keep you from smelling horrid.

Authentic Radicalism: Genuine passion and power to make changes and improvements through positive disruptive beliefs and action. Git 'er done!

Chemical Free: When fabrics, detergents, and natural fiber farming are free of toxic horribleness.

Circular Economy: An entire economy (production and consumption of goods and services) based on the buying and selling of products that can be recycled and reused over and over and over again.

Clean Production: Making things without "f"ed up stuff in them! Healthy!

Closed Loop: Creating items starting with thinking of how they can be reused again and again. Post consumer products are used to make the same new products (Example: a used cotton T-shirt is recycled to make another new cotton T-shirt).

Conscious Consumerism: Shoppers who give a shift and buy stuff accordingly

Cradle to Cradle: Creating an item with the idea that it can be made into something else for eternity, or at least for a really long time. Similar to closed loop and circular economy, cradle to cradle is looking at the product lifecycle from the start (cradle) to manufacturing, use, end of life (grave), and back to start (cradle).

Cradle to Grave: The alternative to cradle to cradle – something that is intentionally made to be broken, so that you will have to buy it again and again. It is not intentionally made to be broken down. It is a term used in lifecycle assessment to draw a boundary around which emissions are to be considered in the study.

Creative Economy: An entire economy (production and consumption of goods and services) based on the buying and selling of products made by turning unique individuals ideas into sellable items.

DIY: Do it yo'self. Otherwise known as a 'chop shop' in fashion. (Trashing T-shirts is great for stress and anxiety. You can take out your aggression and get creative at the same time.)

Disruptors: The more accurate, innovative, and empowering term to describe an activist. Get shi(f)t done kind of people!

Endocrine Disruptors: Chemicals that have been found to "f" up the flow of your body and possibly cause cancer.

Ethical Labor: Treating workers with respect and providing them with the means to have a respectful style of life.

Fair Trade: "Fair," meaning to be treated kindly, paid enough to eat well, live healthy lives and celebrate special occasions. Golden rule stuff: Treat others as you'd want to be treated. "Trade," as in, I choose to trade my dollars for your product. We kind of like the saying: "Vote with your dollars," but it doesn't always resonate. Trade, however, is more like: "I'll trade you this Iron Man toy for your Wonder Woman toy," arguably an even trade. Most uneducated shoppers are trading their Spider-Man action figure for a piece of poop. It's gross, and definitely not a "fair" trade.

Fast Fashion: Cheap clothes and accessories that are made to break quickly so that you shop more. It creates waste and is often made by treating people and the planet in unspeakable ways.

Greenwashing: A misleading perception to make something look eco-friendly, but is really sneaky. I think it's called bait-and-switch.

Local Production: Clothes produced by locals to create jobs for locals. Supporting local economies help communities, cities and whole counties thrive. It's a great way to learn about, and sometimes even meet, the makers. Farm to Fashion. Artisans. Craftspeople.

Local Sourcing: When finding fabrics, trims, and other goods within a local (let's estimate 100-mile) radius of a company.

Makers: People who make stuff. These are humans who have an idea and execute it, often inviting other creative people to help them in the process.

Mending: This is literally just patching holes! How many other ways can we say: "STOP THROWING CLOTHES IN THE TRASH!". H&M intentionally sews with long stitches so that tops get holes in seams more easily. Sew that shit up!

Microfibers: The tiny fibers that make up the ball of fabric you pull off a dryer's lint trap. When rinsed down a drain, in your washer for example, they can cause serious issues when set free in the oceans. So, why don't washers also have lint traps? Someone needs to do something about that, like NOW.

Mindful Luxury: Expensive stuff that takes all aspects of the supply chain into consideration. Mindfully-made luxury items respect the humans that made them and respects the planet throughout the growing, manufacturing, and distribution processes.

Mordants (fixative): Metals in the form of a salt that attach dyes to fibers. (When dyeing an organic fiber, research the mordant, because it may be more toxic than the fiber and the dye.)

Over-production: When a brand knows that they can sell an item for several different price points, high in the store at the mall, medium online, and low at an outlet mall to cover costs! Sometimes unbuyable clothing gets burned or shipped overseas. No one wants our shitty excess, so let's encourage large brands to produce less and be more specific about what they supply in the stores.

○ **Yay! The rush you get at an outlet mall when buying a $15 pair of over-produced jeans adds to a broken system of excessive textile waste. The rush you get when paying $15 at a vintage store for even higher quality jeans, while helping to reduce waste, and not cause waste, is a far more fabulous high!**

Planned Obsolescence: When an item is made with the intention to break or become unfashionable in a specific amount of time – short enough that the shopper will need to buy it multiple times, and long enough that they'll still trust the company or person who made it.

Post-Consumer Waste: Items that have come to the end of their lives and have been used by a shopper. People who haven't read this guidebook would consider a plastic bottle to be trash. Innovative people utilize the plastic bottle as a resource to create something new.

Pre-Consumer Waste: Items that have come to the end of their lives that have not been used by a shopper. For example, when fabric is cut to make clothing, the cutting scraps from around the pattern have usually been discarded. Innovative people take the waste fabric, grind it up, and make it into new fabric.

Rayon: Conventionally, the rayon fabric-making process is caustic and toxic. In the 80's rayon, equated to luxury, in the 2010's it equates to danger. Beware of harsh chemical processing.

Recycled PET: Discarded plastic that gets ground up, mashed into pellets, and then made into solid plastic items and fabrics.

Recycled Fabric: Cutting scraps and secondhand clothes that are ground up and made into new, soft, durable fabrics that reduce waste.

Recycled Plastic Bottle Fabric: Made by shredding post-consumer plastic bottles, which are then made into pellets, pushed through spindles, and woven or knit into fabric.

Recycling Clothing: Textiles can be recycled just like glass, plastic, and paper. (Donate to charity organizations. Trade in your old pieces at stores like Crossroads and Buffalo Exchange. Drop garments in I:CO bins at your local mall. See if your city has a clothing recycling program. Direct any other questions to WearDonateRecycle. org.)

<u>Slow Fashion:</u> Handcrafted fashion pieces made with intention that pay attention to detail in each part of the process in an old-timey, crafty, give a shift, DIY kind of way. Mix and matchable classic, durable pieces often live longer in your closet.

<u>Sustainable Fabrics:</u> Awesome fabrics that are made mindfully so they don't harm people or the planet; fabrics that are not doused with toxic chemicals. Consider supporting fabric innovations you vibe with. If you know or love a designer, get pleasantly pushy and ask for better fabrics: recycled, biodegradable, and/or chemical- free. Support fabric manufacturers that kick ass in the "we give a shift" department. Read labels. Transparency rules! Certifications justify.

<u>Upcycled Clothing:</u> Trash to treasure! For example, bicycle tires, fire hoses, and discarded chip bags can be made into wallets, bracelets, and belts.

<u>Vegan Fashion:</u> Clothing that doesn't utilize any animal parts or byproducts in its making. This also means no wool and no silk. (Boiling silkworms to remove the thread from their dead bodies is monstrous!)

<u>Waste Culture:</u> Our current fashion manufacturing system does not work. All fashion eventually comes to the end of its lifecycle. These days, some people go through 10 articles of clothing per month or per year. On average, Americans toss 80 pounds of clothing per year. Readers/shoppers: Let's each take it upon ourselves to recycle 10 articles of clothing, and make sure they're properly recycled into a new textile. Designers: think about how the fabrics you choose are made and what happens to it when the item of clothing meets its end.

<u>Waterless Cotton:</u> Conventionally grown cotton for denim and T-shirts uses a bazillion gallons of water globally. Waterless cotton uses less water. There are new technologies that reduce water during the growing process, the washing, the dying, and the finishing.

<u>Zero Waste:</u> One of the best examples we can think of to demonstrate this concept and practice is through a pattern-cutting process, where someone gets really creative and jigsaws each subsequent cut so that literally no waste is left over at the end. Everything is used! Shoppers can practice zero waste by avoiding mass amounts of packaging and buying items that are made to be recycled over and over.

> *"Once you learn about what's going on and how much **suffering exists** for the people and the **planet** through the **manufacturing** of our **clothing**, it's hard to not change your shopping habits. There are some things that **you can't unsee.**"*
>
> *– Lisa Mazzotta, producer of RiverBlue documentary*

BEYOND THE LABEL RECAP OF THE WEAR YOUR VALUES EVENT BY BTL TEAM MEMBER AUDREY STANTON

This past Fashion Revolution Week went out with a bang over on the west coast! Los Angeles hosted a myriad of exciting events and the Wear Your Values pop up and panel was no exception. On April 28th, at Row DTLA, shoppers, advocates, and designers alike gathered in the name of conscious fashion. Galerie.LA, along with Remake, Triarchy, Conscious Chatter, Fashion Revolution USA, and Beyond the Label partnered to share multiple sustainable vendors, interactive displays, and educational videos. Brands inside Galerie. LA include Triarchy, HFS Collective, and Study N.Y. Brands such as Mate the Label, Back Beat Rags, and Soko gathered outside the sustainable shop to share their designs with guests. It was a sea of beautiful patterns, organic fabrics, and innovative ideas.

Beyond the Label was proud to present educational videos, to share the power, passion, and purpose of Industry of All Nations, RiverBlue, and Patagonia - a video about their Worn Wear program. Worn Wear is a program put forth by Patagonia to recycle garments we already have. When you send in used items from the brand, they will give you a credit to trade in for another gently used item and the cycle goes on and on from there. (Worn Wear also has a mobile van which has partnered with Fashion Revolution in the past to mend clothes on location while touring the U.S.).

*A table featuring the Beyond the Label's first edition of the How to Shop for Shi(f)t guidebook was available for purchase and BtL team members gathered to discuss how to **#MakeShiftHappen** with attendees. The guidebook is a detailed consumer guide to shopping more sustainably, no matter what your buying practices are.*

Following the wonderful mingling and shopping was a panel moderated by Conscious Chatter's Kestrel Jenkins. Dechel Mckillian, Ayesha Bartenblat, and Adam Taubenfligel discussed the progress that the conscious fashion community has made, and the feats still to come. Designers, curators, and changemakers alike have different, yet essential, roles in this movement we call slow fashion. The takeaway? Camaraderie is key in this industry because we cannot make lasting change without each other. By sticking together we can, and will have a fashion revolution.

Event: *Galerie.LA "Wear Your Values" REMAKE*
Panelists/Partners: *Kestrel Jenkins/Conscious Chatter (moderator), Ayesha Barenblat/Remake, Dechel Mckillian/Galerie.LA, Adam Taubenfligel/Triarchy*
Beyond the Label *participated with immersive, educative installations. BtL shared short films: Patagonia, RiverBlue, and Industry of All Nations. Fashion Revolution USA represented, yay!*

Galerie.LA - DTLA (Los Angeles)

FASH REV MIAMI 2018

MIAMI'S FIRST COLLECTIVE FASHION REVOLUTION EVENT
RECAP BY NATHALIA ORQUERA

*This year Fashion Revolution Miami, was an extension of the first ever event that took place in Miami in 2017 to bring awareness of **"Who made your Clothes"**. It was a no brainer that all the local ethical fashion designers and entrepreneurs wanted to unite to continue spreading the message of sustainability and transparency in the fashion industry. From the original group of five, Krel Wear, Trunk Collective, The Onikas, Shop Suspiro, The Full Edit, many more joined the conversation and festivities. There is a growing community in Miami willing to promulgate the message locally but also to the Latin Countries, as Miami is the getaway to reach all of them.*

*The central theme for the Fashion Revolution event this year was the Circular Economy - to bring awareness of how clothes are made and how to properly dispose of them at the end of life. There was a very lively and debated panel where guests enthusiastically asked questions from how to create an ethical wardrobe to how to recycle clothes. The main event was the clothing swap organized in conjunction with **Global Fashion Exchange**. Guests brought up to 6 items of gently used clothes to be swap for something they will use and cherish even more. We wanted to encourage guests to see the value of "pre-loved" clothes, that they are not "hand me downs", but as an alternative to renew their closets without spending a dime or hurting the environment or garments workers. It was great to see the smiles on people's faces when they got rid of their unused clothes, and left excited with their new finds for a whole new outfit. This way we can dispel the stigma that second hand clothes carries in Latam countries. A portion of the remaining clothes were donated to charity (Lotus House) and clothes that were no longer wearable were to be upcycled or recycled by the Nomad Tribe store.*

Guests had the opportunity to shop ethically made clothes and accessories by local designers and engage one on one with them and learn the stories behind the people who makes their products. Some of the brands work with artisans in Ecuador, India, Uganda, Bolivia, and Guatemala and one can easily trace where the products come from. This way we can inspire guests and shoppers to always question who made their clothes and where they come from. Brands participating included Antidote, Sonder & Holiday, Suspiro Handbags, The Onikas, Krel Wear, Carolina K, The Full Edit, and author of "The cheat sheet of Italian Style" Francesca Belluomini.

Event: *Fashion Revolution Miami*
Organizer: *Nathalia Orquera of Maria Loves Green*
Panelists: *Colleen Coughlin/The Full Edit (moderator) Sophie Zembra/Antidote Store, Karelle Levy/KrelWear, Veronica Pesantes/The Onikas, Valeria Savino/ Nomad Tribe Store*
Brands/Sponsors: *Antidote, Carolina K, KrelWear, Nomad Tribe, Suspiro Handbags, Sonder & Holliday, The Onikas, The Full Edit, and Francesca Belluomini author of "The Cheat Sheet of Italian Style", Villa Riviera sustainable wine, Sharron Lewis Design Center/Factory.*

Sharron Lewis Design Center - Miami

FASHION REVOLUTION WEEK EVENTS IN NYC (15+ events total) RECAP BY VLOGGER BENITA ROBLEDO

Up until a few years ago, I thought machines did most of the work. I mean we have self-driving cars now, they should be able to do everything right? Wrong. Robots may be able to open doors, but they can't sew seams for shit.

WHAT YOU CAN DO ABOUT IT
After a week of my emotions bouncing back and forth from joy because of all our progress and horror at how far we had to go, I'm left with this. We can't let Fashion Revolution Week be the only time we put pressure on companies and governments to change. Most Fashion Revolutionaries will encourage you take action by writing a letter to a company or tweeting about it. Yes, do this definitely. But if you're anything like me, you'll start out super gung-ho and quickly burn out because you know...life. Letters and pics will only get us so far. The revolution is a marathon, not a sprint, and we must make small choices day in and day out if we want change to last. We must vote with our dollar every single day. Luckily, this is easier than it sounds. These three actions will help keep brands honest.

1. Buy Fair-trade. *This is the number one way to ensure workers are treated fairly and make a decent wage from their work.*

2. Buy Union-made. *Unions have their workers backs. It's their job! Unions not only protect its members but by raising standards improve the lives of all workers.*

3. Buy Less, But Buy Better. *One of the biggest hurdles to in this whole ethical production cycle is us. What are we the consumer willing to spend on an item. Since the Rana Plaza collapse the price of men's pants have dropped 13%. Since the Rana Plaza collapse the price of men's pants have dropped 13%. How the hell are factories supposed to pay their workers a living wage, when we expect to pay next to nothing? Where is that money supposed to come from?*

Event: *BFDA - FR Launch Night Open Studio*
Panelists: *Amy Dufault (moderator), Tara St. James, Austin Lee (FR USA Rep), BFDA participants*

Event: *Parsons - How Can Fashion Change the World*
Panelists: *Anurag Jain (moderator), Abrima Erwiah/Studio One Eighty Nine, Stephanie Benedetto/Queen of Raw, Tabitah St. Bernard/Livari, Tara St. James/ Study NY, Leonardo Bononni/Sourcemap*

Event: *Fashion Revolution USA "Insight Into a Changing Landscape"*
Panlists: *Celine Semaan/SlowFactory (moderator), Shivam Punjya/Benho, Mara Hoffman/Mara Hoffman, Kristen Schneider/Nest, Amanda Curtis/ NineteenthAmendment*

Event: *Stella McCartney, The RealReal, and Fashion Revolution*
Panelists: *A discussion with Stella McCartney's head of sustainability Claire Bergkamp & the RealReal director of women's category Sasha Skoda*

For Fashion Revolution Week 2018 there were 80 events across 20 cities!

BFDA - Brooklyn Fashion + Design Accelerator

Parsons - NYC

Fashion Revolution - NYC

Stella McCartney - SOHO

BtL o LIBS

CALL TO ACTION BTL LIBS

DEAR ______________,
PERSON IN CHARGE
(Ex. CEO/Head of Production)

I went to your store because I needed a ______________
POSITIVE ADJ
(Ex. Organic/recycled fabric)

______________ and all I could find was ______________, which
ITEM OF CLOTHING   NEGATIVE DESCRIPTOR
(Ex. Dress/underwear)   (Ex. Toxic dyed, petroleum-based)

______________.
DEROGATIVE EXPLANATION
(Ex. Sucks/is unacceptable)

Please let me know when you will be selling items for

customers like myself. If I'm asking for a ______________
POSITIVE ADJ LISTED ABOVE

______________, then I believe others would like to buy it too.
ITEM LISTED ABOVE

Thanks in advance for considering taking your ______________
POSITIVE SHOPPER ADJ
(Ex. Ecocurious/awesome)

customers as well as the health of your ______________ clothing
POSITIVE THOUGHT PROVOKING ADJ
(Ex. Hardworking, Perservering)

makers into consideration when buying ______________
POSITIVE ADJ LISTED ABOVE

______________ to stock your store.
ITEM LISTED ABOVE

Most graciously and gratefully, ______________
SUPER EXCITED NOUN
(Ex. Shopaholic, Sustainable Shopping Enthusiast)

T

THANK YOUS

THANK YOU, THANK YOU, THANK YOU:

Core team and key players: Thank you to everyone that contributed quotes to this guidebook! We appreciate your brain and awesomeness. To Kritika Misra of GOOD Magazine, Caroline Pham, our fabulous editors, and all of our esteemed beta testers (you know who you are – hugs), Miss Lauren Selman for encouraging the original creation of EcoDivas, The BtL Team: Karen Housel, Nicholas J. Brown, Allison Sherman, Maggie Pa, Audrey Stanton, Naomi Goez, Veronica Ko, Tiffany Wong, Juana Baltazar, Swati Panchal, Julia Jaye Posin, and Janell Hipwell. And the OG BtL Team: Robin Shirley, Jeanie You, Alisa Kharikyan, Sinjun, Nikkia Sipes, Erin Brown, Melissa Flewelling, Alexander Hoyt, and anyone who has ever volunteered for a Beyond the Label event including fashion show dressers, makeup artists, models, and photographers – we as a team appreciate your support!

Beyond the Label launch supporters: Syama Meagher, Amir Banifatemi, and Eric Espinosa of TEDxLA, FBI (Fashion Business Inc.), Ashleigh Kaspszak of the New Mart, Andrew Morgan Director/Producer of *The True Cost*, Shona Quinn Sustainability Lead at Eileen Fisher, Kathleen Talbot Sustainability and Business at Reformation, Susanna Schick Founder of Sustainable Fashion LA, Guyaki (Yerba Mate) for their transparent positive sustainable business model, Textile Insight Magazine (my first writing gig), Dechel Mckillian of Galerie.LA, and all of the designers and experts who have participated in breakout circles. I'd also like to thank everyone that has attended and contributed to BtL's #MakeShiftHappen movement and to my mom, dad, sis, bro, gma and fam.

Fabulous mentors: David Zucker, Mark Sagato, Georgia Berner, Sass Brown, Connie Ulasewicz, Penn Collins, the UCLA Social Enterprise Academy facilitators, and Paul Levitz (for initially telling me to read *Skinny Bitch* and encouraging me to write with sass).

Schools, events, and organizations: Dylan Kendall (formerly Hollywood Media & Arts), Kami Cotler and Allison Diaz of Environmental Charter High School, Roni Miller and Kristine Upesleja of FIDM, Sass Brown (formerly FIT), Joshua Williams of FIT, Lorrie Ivas of Santa Monica College, Gina Garcia of Sustainable Works, Milton Hernandez of Sourcing at MAGIC, Sonali Diddi of Colorado State University, Net Impact Pepperdine & UCLA, Billy Lombe of Youth Environmental Network Zambia, Puni Hamir of Namanunga School Lusaka Zambia, and schools, events, and organizations that have given Beyond the Label, EcoDivas, and myself a platform to shout from the rooftops! THANK YOU!

And thank YOU for taking the time to read this guidebook and taking in the things that resonate with you. **#MakeShiftHappen**

– Taryn Hipwell

APPENDIX